The Master:

Love, Latitude, Longitude, & Laughter

Happy sailing!
Jan Ferris Koltun

Jan Ferris Koltun

ISBN 9781483504544

Printed in USA by Bookbaby.com

Preface

Of the 2,497 Liberty ships delivered during World War II, it is estimated that 229 were lost. The remainder were scrapped or sold to other countries after the war. To write about my father, I discovered, was to write about ships and people no longer on this planet, even in most of our long-term memories.

I am grateful to everyone who helped me to refresh these memories, especially to my mother, who spent her later years trying to make sense out of the books, papers and memorabilia that she and my father accumulated through the decades. She's the celebrity of this book.

"I want to deal with this so you won't have to," she'd say when my husband and I, and our children, visited in the summers, and when I was caring for her in her later years.

Now I've come to that stage myself, still competing with my mother to clean up the mess. This may never happen to the degree I'd like, but it has been a joy to bring clarity to my limited understanding of her husband's--my father's--life.

I'm immensely grateful to her, and to everyone who has helped with this book: Nancy Alexander; Louise and Richard Boone; Sara Brewer; Joyce Burghardt, Dick, Galen Jr., and Patty Burghardt; Carol Clark; Danny Davis; Bob Eagan and "Captain Josephine;" Carol, Jim, Geri, and Bob Ellis; Molly Franklin; Sharon Greer; Jeff Hull; James Huntoon; Chris and Evelyn Jensen; Virginia Jensen, Capt. Robert Johnson; Tish Knapp; John, Joe, Ellen, Gabriella and Calvin Koltun; Susan Kunk; Jim and Nola Long; Matson Navigation Company; Lin McNulty; Brita Merkel; Susan Mustard; Gene Nery; Fred Nicol; Jim Nicol, Eva and Corky North; Greg Plunges; Jeannine and Bob Rodenberger; Joseph Sanchez; Mary Schoen; Bud Shortridge; Carole Speight; Jack Titus; Monique Turner; Ginnie Vitiniamalo.; and the entire, patient staffs of AppleCare and Pages.com.

Table of Contents

Dedication

To mariners everywhere

Foreword

To paraphrase Oscar Wilde; "Children begin by loving their parents; as they grow older they judge them; sometimes, [if they're lucky], they forgive them. This book emerged because all three--loving, judging, and forgiving--have occurred. I'm certain that all three also enter into the development of passion and joy. May the same fortune happen for you!

Chapter One: Daydreams

When someone fully masters a career, art, or skill, many lives are influenced, not only in one lifetime but down through the centuries. My father, an American master mariner, accomplished this through daydreams, nightmares, and turbulent actions.

How does an individual develop a passion to master a career or an art? How does that passion become a life-long pursuit? The life of Captain Harold Benjamin Ferris (HBF), a stew of love, compass points, and laughter, became a commitment that has touched many other lives.

Today, more than a hundred years after HBF was born, the boy whom he mentored is a senior Columbia River bar pilot, bringing ships from all over the world across that tumultuous bar. His protégé's daughter, who now owns Dad's sextant, is on her way to Mumbai on a container ship. When she graduates next year from the U.S. Merchant Marine Academy, she wants to captain a tall ship. I have chosen to write about life because he and my mother instilled my understanding that this is important.

Capt. Ferris (1903-1985), was a short man who dreamed tall. His curly hair remained blond—with one week's exception —even as he grew stout in his later years. His passion for mastery absorbed him, whether he was piloting a ship or an airplane, teaching a pet crow to pull a cigarette from a pack, or painting a roof.

Having a passion for mastery didn't always mean success at what he was trying to master. My mother and I once came home from church to find him sitting in the front yard with an enormous paint bucket over his head. He'd painted clear down to the roof's edge before
finding, to his surprise, there were no more shingles to paint. It took us a week to get all the green paint out of his hair.

No record exists of what he said on that occasion, but he had phrases that family members and friends still use. For instance driving on freeways, a missed exit was always a "must-was," defined as a place where you *must* get off, which *was* at least a few miles back when you noticed the oversight. When a family member displays hubris, he or she may be reminded of Dad's aphorism, "Couldn't stand prosperity."

Old-timers of Orcas Island, part of the San Juan Archipelago in Washington State, still recall HBF helping to open a new bar at Bartel's Resort by standing on a table to recite the full 23 verses of the ballad, "Yarn of the Nancy Bell," [1] or flying his Stinson past the stone tower atop Mt. Constitution and skimming the treetops down its north slope, or landing his yellow Aeronca on docks next to his ships moored in Seattle or Portland.

He was born in Benton Harbor, Michigan, in 1903, the year of Charlotte Perkins Gilman's celebrated study of women's roles, *The Home: Its Work and Influence,* and W.E.B. Du Bois' *The Souls of Black Folk,* a central work of their century's African-American social freedom movement. I like to think, but somehow doubt, that HBF would be pleased that American women now can become sea captains; he was shocked and irate in the early Fifties when he docked in Bombay next to a Russian ship captained by--God forbid!--a female. HBF would have benefited from reading either book.

Although HBF was born on May 13, 1903, the earliest formal photographs of the new arrival were made about nine months later, when he was all decked out in his christening robes. The family was Methodist. The infant, who already looked fully in command of his world, joined two older brothers, Frank and Chester. Although their lives were comparatively bland, they enjoyed each other's company and as adults were good friends.

---

[1] The ballad, about cannibalism, is told as a first-hand story by a "weedy and long" old man who has survived a shipwreck.

Top of page: Harold Benjamin Ferris, 9 months; below: Benjamin and Evelyn Ferris

MIDDLETOWN, OHIO, 1907--Chester (top left), Frank, and Harold, the center of attention, a position he retained for most of his life. Of the three brothers, HBF most closely resembled his father.

HBF's father, Benjamin Ferris, an itinerant real-estate entrepreneur, and his wife, Evelyn Nickerson, who had been postmistress in a small southern town before her marriage, were not deeply engaged in politics. She was a sturdy homemaker who made good cake
doughnuts when she moved from "back east" to Orcas Island in her nineties.

Soon after his birth, his family moved to Ada, Ohio, where HBF's childhood was one for which he was nostalgic during his old age. When I gave him a tape recorder one Christmas, for instance, I hoped he would tell some of his sea stories into it. My mother couldn't listen to those tapes during the first year after he died, until she finished mourning. When we did listen we were disappointed; all he talked about was Ada and the neighbors there.

When HBF was about five, in Middletown, Ohio, Benjamin got rid of their horse and carriage. He bought one of Henry Ford's new Model T cars. His sons reported that he couldn't find the brakes, so he drove right through the horse's former barn yelling, "Whoa, goddamit, whoa!" Soon afterwards, he drove his family to Washington, D.C., where some or all of them lived at 4115 Eighth St. N.W. for the next five decades.

Evelyn kept her house with hired help, which in those days would have been entirely black. In her old age, she told with pleasure about going to a cake-walk when invited by her housekeeper.

Evelyn adored traveling, whether with her husband on his frequent business trips to Florida or visiting her sister, Nan, in 1924 in Jefferson Island, Montana, where she rode a horse while her youngest son was becoming an Able-Bodied Seaman

on the Admiral Fiske, a West Coast cargo vessel.

Harold began to develop his passion on the Potomac River, a few miles from their home. As an old man, he reminisced: "From the improvised crow's nest on top of the woodshed in our back yard, at age six I sighted the Island of Whatnot. It was a beautiful little atoll so I landed a crew and made some interesting explorations. . . I never quite shook myself from these dreams of my childhood. I became a wharf rat on the Potomac even though our home was a good five miles from that part of town. During summer vacations I worked on anything that floated on these waters."

HBF was impressed by such vessels as President Taft's yacht Mayflower, which plied the Potomac as the home of much diplomacy. Acquired during the Spanish-American War, it had been recommissioned by Theodore Roosevelt to house delegates to the 1905 conference that ended the Russo-Japanese War.

More important to HBF's life, however, was another event initiated by President Roosevelt: the opening of the Panama Canal. On August 3, 1914, the first ship passed through the new waterway, which had been completed the previous year to eliminate the perilous, expensive trip around South America.

Chester, Frank and Harold agreed on the fact that their father wouldn't pay for college after they graduated from Central High School. This was a disappointment for three bright young men. HBF joked about having graduated from the "U. of H.K.," or "University of Hard Knocks." His brothers became civil servants. HBF had different goals in mind.

He wanted to be near the ocean. During high school, he'd been working as a driving instructor, which led to a job chauffeuring a professor up to New England while teaching him how to drive. There, HBF's daydreams expanded with the discovery of Maine's small, rocky islands. He photographed them, wrote on the backs of all the photos. This love of islands was enhanced more than a decade later when he visited a dozen atolls in the South Pacific, and then discovered Orcas Island, Washington.

Apparently the professor learned to drive, because by the fall of 1920 the 17-year-old Harold was looking for a place to live and a job in Boston, with a scant $2 in his pocket. He tried the YMCA on Huntington Avenue. The desk clerk steered him to a rooming house on nearby Gainsborough Street.

He lived on beans and bread, at 25 cents a plate, for a couple of days, until he found a job washing dishes on the Eastern Steamship Company's excursion vessel Camden, which ran between Boston and Camden, Maine.

In the galley, he managed to "get a few wrinkles out of my belly" while beginning to learn important elements of mastery: job structure and control.

The shipping company employed four men to wash dishes and polish silver. The dishwashing job was the more difficult labor. HBF was surprised to be assigned the silver-cleaning work. Soon, he found out why he'd been given the job that looked easier. When the galley was closed down at the end of each trip, the trio on dish detail were off within 20 minutes, while the silver cleaner had to stick around for another hour to polish, count, and stow the silver.

For all that, plus buying his own foul-weather gear, his wages were $45 a month. When the tourist season ended, so did that job.

He'd managed to save $30. That allowed him to return to the Gainsborough Street rooming house, a fine economic solution for young people getting started on their careers. They relished every opportunity to eat.

There he met a man he called "Ed," who was employed. They took a room together to cut down on the overhead. Soon, however, Ed lost his job.

On Saturday night, with less than a dollar between them, they scammed another roomer, Al, who wanted to sell a typewriter to raise $5 "for a date he hoped to keep."

HBF offered $4, which neither he nor Ed possessed.

When Al brought them the machine, the pair told him they needed to try it out before paying him. Al went to take a shower. When they heard the water running, they hauled the typewriter to the nearest pawnshop. They pocketed $9 for it and made it back to pay Al his $4.

While he was broke, HBF discovered another important component of mastery: being qualified to do a job. If one dreamed of doing anything, he needed expertise. A little chutzpah didn't hurt either.

In Scollay Square's Pioneer Market, he found an ad for a part-time butcher. He talked his way into the job, which paid a whopping $11 for one Saturday.

"It never occurred to me that I knew less than nothing about butchery," he wrote many years later. "A job was being offered. I said I'd take it. The manager looked me over and said, 'You look too damn young to be much of a butcher.'

"I looked him right in the eye and said 'I'm asking for the job. Do you want a butcher or don't you?' He said, 'Be here at six in the morning.'"

The next day he was shivering in the market doorway when the head butcher arrived. Asked where his tools were, HBF said he'd had to hock them. The manger took him to the basement, lent him an outsized white coat, some knives and a whetstone, and pointed at one of ten cutting blocks.

"You take block number five and go into box number two. Get a rack of fores and bone 'em," he ordered.

HBF said he found the box but had no idea what he was supposed to do. "All I could do was stand around and try to fish something out of my subconscious mind that had never been there," he recalled.

Soon he learned from another temporary helper that his assignment was to bone forequarters of lamb and make them up into rolls. He tried to watch the co-worker whet his knives, bone lamb and tie up the rolls. He concluded: "the lamb was either deformed to start with or a contortionist who died during his act."

An hour later the manager called HBF into his office to ask why he had palmed himself off as a meat cutter. When told the truthful answer, that he'd needed a job, he was allowed to work the rest of the day if he would promise not to return.

At 6 PM, he drew his $11, lifted an apple from the market on his way out, and took the street car back to the rooming house. He shared ham and eggs with his friend Ed. The next day they gave the landlady $5. They were still behind on their rent.

Ingenuity was another precursor of mastery. HBF scoured the Boston docks for a ship. He learned to get by gate watchmen, hired to ward off job applicants during those Depression years, by carrying an envelope addressed to "Chief Officer, S.S. _____."

When he was allowed aboard the vessel to deliver the bogus mail, he could ask others about the availability of work. Thus he found his first ship bound for the West Coast: the American-Hawaiian Company freighter, *Pennsylvanian*.

To his surprise, the Chief Mate said he could use an Ordinary Seaman, and that the vessel was sailing in two hours. If HBF could get his gear on board by then, he could have the job.

"I managed to walk down the gangway. I'm sure that I went into a fast walk out of the dock, but when I hit the street, I ran. I even did the unheard-of and took a taxi back. I was there well under the two hours."

When he returned with his gear, he realized that he hadn't even asked where the ship was bound. Thirty-six hours later, it turned out that the destination was the West Coast of the United States, through President Roosevelt's new canal.

Chapter Two: Studying for Mastery

To fully comprehend a trade, an art, or a profession requires much more than passing exams. Observing and interacting with people, learning who to trust and the extent to which trust will be rewarded, is paramount.

An Ordinary Seaman, as the title implied, was the most inconsequential man on the ship. As a subordinate, dealing with difficult superiors may be the most important milestone on the road to mastery. Young HBF learned this well from the Chief Mate, a "Mr. Bucko," whom he and the other Ordinaries feared.

Upon leaving Boston for the West Coast, the Pennsylvanian headed into a nasty Atlantic storm. HBF recalled that he would have been seasick but he was too scared of Mr. Bucko, whom he described as a "hard case," to let himself think about throwing up.

"Mr. Bucko was one of the few officers of the modern era whom I ever knew to manhandle one of his crew. While he carried a constant threat, he resorted to an actual deed of violence only once," HBF reminisced.

Aboard the Pennsylvanian, the Ordinaries were taught to steer, which HBF already thought he knew from his days on the Potomac. Then they were given their turn on the bridge while the officers had dinner.

Against his early expectations--and all good marine practice since the eighteenth-century days of Capt. James Cook-- there seemed to be no fresh fruit for the crew. As the young Ordinaries climbed the ladder to the bridge they could see, through an open porthole in the Chief Officer's room, a large dish heaped with apples and oranges. When their hands were on the ladder rail, they were within a foot of the dish.

Each day the fruit became more tempting. One evening HBF snatched an apple. He divided it with another Ordinary, Joe, who promised to grab one more when he relieved the wheel the following evening.

After Joe had gone to the bridge, the saloon messman told HBF that Mr. Bucko had told the Captain someone was eating his fruit and he was going to load an apple with croton, a drastic cathartic. Too late, HBF started for the boat deck to warn Joe not to take another apple. Instead of loading the apple, Mr. Bucko had concealed himself inside his room, near the porthole, to await the culprit.

As Joe's arm started through the porthole, his whole body smacked up against the bulkhead. Mr. Bucko had grabbed Joe's arm and given him a sharp pull. Joe, bleeding at the mouth, tumbled to the boat deck. The enraged Mr. Bucko hit Joe between the eyes. As he fell backwards, one of his shoes went over the side. Mr. Bucko didn't strike at him again, but "gave him a lot of bad language concerning his ancestry."

The incident had a happier ending. A few hours later, Mr. Bucko gave Joe one of his own shoes to compensate for the lost one. For the 32 ensuing days until the ship arrived in California, the crew received an apple apiece.

By the time they docked in San Francisco, HBF knew a little about steering a ship, somewhat more about who he could and could not trust. Now he needed further knowledge of the maritime industry's practices. His first concern was figuring out how to ship out again. He soon learned that in those pre-union days, the ship owners controlled the jobs completely.

Anyone wanting to ship out needed to go to the owners' hiring hall on Battery Street, which HBF described as "filthy," stand in line a long time to register, then sit around until his card "got old enough to have the whiskers that would take a job when it came up on the board."

This practice, controlled by the owners in the 1920s but thirteen years later by the unionized work force, has continued in all American shipping. John McPhee, who wrote what modern mariners have called the "epitaph of the U.S. Merchant Marine," described the basics in *Looking for a Ship* (1990):

> The older the card, the better the prospects for a new job. If the card were to go twelve months unused, it would. . . lose all seniority and begin again. In the evolving decline of the United States Merchant Marine, qualified people seeking work so greatly outnumbered the jobs there were to fill that you had to hold a killer card or your chances were slim for shipping out.

In San Francisco, HBF climbed 2,500-foot Mount Tamalpais on foot. Then he discovered that a railroad existed. Looking back, he later commented: "The joke in those days was that the Mt. Tamalpais Railroad was the only thing on the West Coast more crooked than San Francisco City Hall, and that when they dismantled the railroad, it left City Hall in undisputed possession of the title."

Between ships, he could buy ham and eggs, potatoes, toast and coffee for 35 cents, and a clean room with private bath at $7 a week. Even with these reasonable living costs, his finances were running low. By haunting the hiring hall, he picked up an Ordinary Seaman job on the Admiral Fiske, a small cargo vessel which ran up and down the coast between Portland, Oregon, and San Diego. She also carried 60 passengers.

Earlier named Senator, she had been used to transport military in the Spanish-American War. Her top speed was eleven knots in good weather. The unlicensed personnel occupied forward quarters that were frequently damp. HBF worked hard at swabbing decks after rainstorms to prevent slippage of crew, passengers, and cargo, which earned him respect from the Quartermaster and Captain.

He was also beginning to discover that some officers were not as moralistic as the inhabitants of his Methodist home back in D.C. From the time he came aboard the Fiske, he heard Captain Robb described as a "ladies' man." A few months later, he had a first-hand demonstration when the Captain came off watch and entered his quarters through a screen door that opened off the boat deck.

HBF was working on the boat deck when the screen door opened and a female passenger shouted, "Come on, Robb! My husband's in the barber chair; we've got twenty minutes!"

The young Ordinary Seaman was observing all sorts of extraordinary characters, including one who was to fire him on two separate occasions. That was "Mr. Eric," the Fiske's second officer. Trained in his native Australia, he had become a U.S. citizen, obtained an American license, and "was looking for promotion avidly." Although HBF thought his superior had more experience and competence than Capt. Robb, he appeared "sour on life."

About six months after HBF joined the crew, Capt. Robb went on vacation and Mr. Eric became the chief officer. Two weeks after that, Capt. Eric fired HBF for the first time. "He said he didn't want the teacher's pet around. Then just two weeks later I met him on the Embarcadero and he told me to report aboard the next morning," HBF noted.

Capt. Eric was to get his comeuppance from Sven, the Bos'un, who was drunk and belligerent while waiting for the purser to pay him. When the Captain told Sven to pipe down, Sven looked him over and bellowed: "Who the hell are you?" By way of reply Capt. Eric showed his uniformed arm, which bore four stripes indicating his rank.

As Dad saw it, "Sven blinked a couple of times and said 'I just come from uptown where I sees a guy that has gold stripes down his pants legs, gold up and down his arms, and medals all over his chest. He opens the door at the St. Francis Hotel.'

"Capt. Eric turned to the purser and said, 'Fire that man.' The purser turned to Sven and said, 'You're fired.'" Sven stayed in his bunk the rest of the day. The next day, he was on deck as usual, managing his gang despite the altercation.

In 1924 HBF earned his Able-Bodied Seaman's certificate and shipped on the Admiral Fiske again for three months, only to be fired for a second time by Capt. Eric.

After this firing, someone told HBF he could earn big bucks on a steam schooner, a small wooden-hulled lumber carrier, because they paid overtime to the crew for loading lumber. The vessel made about six knots under ideal weather and tide.

Leaving San Francisco, the schooner was left in the wake of the Pacific Steamship Company's flagship, the H.F. Alexander. She was doing 21 knots, bound for Seattle. A day or two later she passed again, going south. Before HBF's vessel reached the Oregon border, the Alexander swished by going north again.

HBF was becoming aware that he needed good equipment and a well-run shipping company. Matson Navigation Company, which had been incorporated in 1901, had the reputation of paying $5 more a month than any of its competitors. The next year, 1925, he earned a certificate of proficiency at managing lifeboats, important for anyone who wanted to work on passenger vessels. In the fall of 1925, at the age of 22, he obtained his first job with the flourishing Matson

Company in Hawai'i.[2] The ship was the first Matsonia, a relatively new vessel, built at Newport News, Virginia, at the beginning of World War I. A plaque indicated that she had borne 34,721 troops to Europe during 1914-18.

The Matsonia carried 240 passengers and a cargo of molasses and sugar on a close schedule between Honolulu, Hilo, and San Francisco. Her Captain was John Diggs, whom HBF described as "a grand gentleman from his toes up through his six-foot-two frame. He could get off a cutting and severe reprimand without getting too far outside of dictionary English, which is a feat for any sea-going man. The occasions for such were very few, and had to have an unquestionably good reason behind them."

HBF viewed the close schedule as an asset. When Matsonia left San Francisco at Wednesday noon on the dot, he knew she was going to tie up at Pier 15 in Honolulu the following Tuesday at 0900. An hour later the watch below could be out on Waikiki Beach. At 1700 on Friday afternoons, they sailed for Hilo. Saturday afternoons, the passengers returned from an overnight tour and a night at Volcano House. Then they returned to Honolulu. Sundays, the crew usually had a free day. On a 28-day turnaround, they sailed from Honolulu again on Wednesday and back to San Francisco the next Tuesday.

The big tourist hotels had not yet been built, but Waikiki offered the young sailors membership in the Outrigger Canoe Club, where thatched-roof sheds provided cover for canoes, surf boards, and wood stoves. Before leaving the ship, each fellow would bum something from the galley, HBF reminisced. "One would get a chunk of meat, another some vegetables or bread. As soon as we got to the beach, we'd start a fire and the Mulligan stew, which we'd eat during the day between surf rides."

At sea, the Quartermasters stood six-hour watches: six on, six off. The two men on the six-to 12 watch got all the dirty

---

2 Matson Navigation Company personnel record, 9/23/25-6/1/68.

*HBF WATER-SKIING OFF WAIKIKI in 1926--A
surfboard served as the single ski, towed behind an
old wooden boat.*

work, such as scrubbing down the bridge and shining the brass, while the 12-to-six watch had it easy. When HBF first joined the Matsonia, he had the more difficult watch; as his experience grew, he could take the easier one.

Steering took up much less time than on older ships, as the Matsonia was one of the first vessels in the Pacific to boast Sperry-Gyro Pilots. With the easier work, HBF decided to start studying for an officer's license.

Homesick for his family back in Washington, D.C. after about eight months, HBF left the Matsonia in San Francisco and took a job as Able-Bodied Seaman with another company. This interlude gave him a lifelong appreciation for Matson's standards.

The new vessel was a Luckenbach ship, on which he signed while thinking it was bound for the East Coast. Later, he found it was going to the Caribbean and back to San Francisco. He found the food terrible, the labor practices monstrous.

On the Matsonia, the unlicensed Quartermasters had worked twelve hours a day. On the Luckenbach vessel, the unlicensed crew put in eight hours a day chipping rust, in addition to eight hours of standing watch. The licensed officers were required to chip rust for four hours plus eight of standing watch.

Observed HBF: "If a chipping hammer stopped for more than a minute, the Chief Officer or the Bos'un was right there to inquire if you had sprained your arm. Even the Captain, stripped to the waist, and all the off-watch officers, hit the boat-anvil chorus before the bridge clock finished striking eight bells to denote the start of the morning watch."

Despite acquiring an enduring dislike for the Luckenbach Line, HBF stayed with them for more trips. He supplemented his salary by purchasing bananas from bumboats in the Panama Canal, then reselling them to the unlicensed crew.

As soon as he could afford it, he spent some time with his family in D.C. Then he headed for the hiring halls of New York, where he was assigned to the President Harding as Quartermaster. He spent some cold four-hour watches, steering in the wintery North Atlantic from an open flying bridge. He also learned more about sharing.

"Before leaving my home in Washington, my brother had insisted that I take a heavy sheep-lined coat with me. At first I was all against it as I didn't think it looked 'sea-doggy' enough. As we got into the colder weather, the coat stood a 24-hour watch every day as it passed from helmsman to helmsman for the entire voyage," he noted.

After three round trips on the President Harding, and a few more voyages to Europe on whatever jobs came up in the hiring halls, HBF found his way back to Hawai'i in 1927. There, he had the good fortune to be assigned as Quartermaster on the SS Maui under Capt. Peter Johnson, the Commodore of the Matson Fleet.

Sometimes HBF griped that his new mentor was a mixed blessing. But as the relationship deepened, it became an incentive to turn him toward intensive study for an officer's license. He also learned another important ingredient of mastery: to turn away from pervasive fears that he couldn't do the work. In his seventies, he reminisced:

> Captain Johnson was one of the last Masters of the Old School. He had been reared in Sail and had to fight a court battle to be allowed to sit for his master's license in Steam. He appeared to be hard as nails and while I never thought for a second that he would rain any kind of physical violence upon me, I was scared of him.
>
> Each trip I figured that he would tell the mate to fire me and sometimes I was so sure of it that I almost quit to beat the rap. He saw all my faults, but didn't waste much time on me. For instance, I'd be at the wheel coming into port, I'd hear a couple of growls because the wheel hadn't responded quickly enough. Just before he left the bridge, he would throw a remark, "Wassamada wid you, you no learn to steer?"

Both men enjoyed playing cribbage and bridge, which helped to narrow the age gap. Soon, HBF found Capt. Peter had "a heart as big as a watermelon." One day, HBF related, he was shining brass on the bridge when the Captain summoned him to announce that Matson was building a new ship at the Cramp Shipyard back in Philadelphia, that HBF should be ready for a license, and "if you can get it, I'm going to give you a junior officer's berth."

Suddenly, everything changed. HBF was still an outsider in Officer Country, but now he had the incentive to study hard.

"I had not obtained the license and had great fears that my mental capacity would not carry the load. But even with 12 hours a day of duty I was able to get in study. I was allowed to stand up and take transit noon day eighth of the meridian transit of the sun. Some days my figures actually agreed with the officers,'" he noted.

His desire for the new ship was so great that he spent his own time and money to go where the action was. Matson wasn't about to pay for a prospective junior officer to go to the East Coast, so he found another intercoastal ship.

He arrived in Philadelphia just in time for the trial run of the new vessel, the Malolo. It turned out to be a maritime disaster in which he distinguished himself before the Matson executives. As a component of mastery, it never hurts to shine during an emergency.

For the Malolo's speed trials off Rockland, Maine, the Cramp Shipyard furnished all the officers and crew. The Matson folk were guests, crowding around the starboard wing of the bridge. On the way up from Philadelphia, near New York, a deep fog set in.

Told to stay out of the way, HBF recounted, he went to the port wing of the bridge, all by himself and "as near invisible as I was able to do without using vanishing cream."

When a whistle sounded off to the port, the shipyard's Captain came out on the wing and announced they were hearing the Nantucket Lightship. It didn't sound like the characteristic signal of the Lightship to anybody who'd been in those waters. HBF had been there years before on the Camden, again on Europe-bound vessels.

The whistle blew again, and a third time. Then, just below HBF's "grandstand position," a long black bow emerged from the fog and entered the hull of the Malolo.

Within seconds, all the VIPs rushed to the port wing. Then, figuring they would watch the bow come out the other side, they rushed to the starboard wing.

The Norwegian ship that had collided with the Malolo was the Jacob Christensen. She had penetrated about 25 feet into the engine room, leaving her starboard anchor on the Malolo's main generator. The other ship had telescoped its bow and never reached Malolo's keel.

Ken Whitelaw, who would become Second Officer of the Malolo when the repairs were eventually made, grabbed HBF and a couple of others. With a flashlight they descended to the F deck, ankle-deep in water. There, they began closing water-tight doors with hand wrenches to prevent the vessel from sinking.

They had to do it by hand because the bridge control for the doors had not been hooked up. Even if they had been, the touted safety controls would have been useless as there was no power in the Malolo after the Jacob Christensen had rammed through the engine room. The dark and scary job had to be done. "All I wanted to do was get the hell out of there. I would have bolted and gotten topside except that Ken Whitelaw had the only flashlight," HBF commented.

A small boat took the Matson folk into New York, where HBF found himself without a job and no pay for the five or six days he'd spent helping to relieve the disaster. Whitelaw assured him he'd have a job when and if the Malolo was ever repaired and the legal problems resolved. For the next six months, HBF needed to find himself another job.

He shipped out as Able-Bodied Seaman on the Army transport Chateau Thiery, bound for the Panama Canal, Hawaiian Islands, and Manila with a load of Army recruits. He liked the Captain, but thought less of the recruits and the way he felt they were treated by the Army brass. "Between the food I saw served to these men, the living conditions and the plain bull-shit that the officers threw at them daily, I wondered how much hunger I would have to endure before I'd need to be beaten down enough to join the Army," he concluded.

He later extended this aversion to the Navy and military in general. Nonetheless, he returned with the rank of Quartermaster.

When he arrived back in New York, he found the Malolo was at Morse Shipyard, two blocks down the street from the Chateau Thiery's Army dock. For the next month, he manned a gangway watch on the graveyard shift for the Thiery, which gave him time to study for the dreaded Third Mate's licensing exam. Matson put him on the payroll with limited day duties.

When the Malolo was nearly repaired, Captain Peter Johnson asked HBF if he had obtained his license. He had not but was ready, he said, to take the exam.

Privately, he had his doubts, but he kept them to himself at the time. When he was old, he recalled:

I hadn't known any greater fear in my life than the day I walked into the office of the Steamboat Inspection Service in New York. The Inspector who was conducting examinations had a long goatee and very fishy eyes. I carried my own Bowditch [the navigational Bible] into the exam room. He grabbed it and shook it with the open leaves upside-down, to see that I had no illegal notes concealed within the pages. (Thank God I'd pasted them all in place.)

I made a few mistakes but he allowed me to correct them after telling me the correct answers, so by the fourth day he looked quite human. On the fifth day I got my Third Mate's license. All the way back to the ship I kept asking myself, "How could a stupid SOB like you get a license?"

Never before or since then had I ever seen Captain Peter Johnson at the sign-on or pay-off of crew, but there he was. He said to the Shipping Commissioner, "Sign dis man on as Junior Third Officer."

The Commissioner looked at me and said, "Do you have a license?" Before I could answer Captain Peter said, "Of course he has." Then he walked out of the room.

The commissioner looked at the date on my "ticket," which was, of course, the day that we were signing on. He asked the Purser for a blotter and then proceeded to blot all over my license, sort of an insulting way of indicating that the ink wasn't dry on my ticket yet.

Of course, acquiring a mentor, studying, exams and experience all are aspects of mastery. But as crucial as any of these is mastery over foes. He'd done well in managing a formidable foe--his fears of the early exams--but many more of these awaited him in 1927. Another enemy still lurked, all the more dangerous because HBF regarded this opponent as a friend. Its name was "alcohol."

This unrecognized foe first showed up during Prohibition, on the Malolo's maiden voyage to the West Coast and Hawai'i.

From New York, with a full complement of well-heeled passengers, the Malolo dropped down to Havana, where there was no shore leave for the crew. Great amounts of booze were brought out in small boats. Matson executives bought many cases of liquor, which were brought out in a barge and stored in a lower hold.

The VIPs argued over the wisdom of this liquor purchase. At Panama, lumber was brought aboard. The crew received overtime pay--unheard-of in Matson--for boxing up the cases of alcohol.

As the Malolo headed up the West Coast in the warm weather, the portholes leading to the bridge were left open. Standing watch, HBF, the junior Third Mate, had an earful of the ongoing discussions. "They all claimed to regret having the illegal booze aboard, but were riding the tiger," he noted.

Soon, a radiogram arrived from the West Coast head of prohibition enforcement, declining a previously-accepted invitation for lunch aboard ship in San Diego. Then HBF heard his mentor tell the President of Matson, the Chairman of the Board of Directors, the Captain of the ship, and other brass, that if they chose to break the law by keeping the liquor on board, he, Capt. Peter, was making his final voyage.

"It took a lot of guts for him to lay it on the table. He won," HBF observed.

Plans were made to dump the cases while the passengers were having dinner. The officers were called to oversee that no booze would be sidetracked by the crew. But when the liquor was delivered on deck, six of the unlicensed engine crew, the "black gang," grabbed a case apiece and fled.

With the three junior officers, including HBF, in pursuit, the black gang lugged the cases through the main dining salon, heading for their quarters near the stern. An additional 30 cases were found on another deck, behind a door barred with three locks.

"Mr. Whitelaw, the Second Mate, reorganized the guards. The rest of Operation Dump was accomplished as planned with the Mexican coastline looming up in the bright moon. The cases looked like chunks of ice floating in a glassy wake," HBF observed.

He had figured out that cases of Scotch would float! This prefigured an incident, 30 years later, when similar cases were dumped from another Matson ship, the Sierra, between Orcas Island and British Columbia. Old Orcas residents still remember departing in a flotilla of small boats to recover the loot from a ship that had been draped in toilet paper so the boaters could recognize it. (See Chapter Six).

After the booze was all dumped, the night before Armistice Day in 1927, HBF and the other junior officers were instructed to walk through the passageway near the crew's quarters, to look around, but not to make a formal search. Then the three men were to report back that there was nothing in sight and that no one seemed drunk.

"When I went to my room, under my pillow were two quarts of Scotch. The Tooth Fairy had been around," the junior Third Officer recorded.

After arrival at San Francisco, Capt. Johnson retired, but rode on to Honolulu, his home port. The Malolo made this leg of her maiden voyage in slightly under four days. Thereafter, she made the turnaround trip in 14 days.

After that trip to the islands and back to San Francisco, HBF was transferred to one of Matson's largest freighters, the Manukai, in the sugar trade from the Hawaiian Islands to the

East Coast. Capt. Charles Morgan was Master. With the transfer came a promotion to Third Mate, which meant he was in charge of a watch.

He studied how his superiors worked. He was impressed by Capt. Morgan's quick display of seamanship one particular night, off the easternmost point of Cuba, when on HBF's watch he discovered that the barometer had jumped up 30 percent in less than an hour. He called down the tube to the Captain's stateroom to report the dramatic rise.

"Reverse the course," Capt. Morgan snapped back. Quickly, he came up to the chart room, squinted at the barometer, and grunted, "That's a hurricane."

The Manukai ran back around the Cuban point into good weather, but began to receive hurricane reports and news of distressed shipping to the south. By noon the next day, they turned north again. The hurricane had swept out into the Atlantic, leaving only long swells and cloudy skies.

HBF studied for successive licenses. A year later, he was promoted to senior Third Mate aboard the second Matsonia. He stayed for six months, until he was promoted to Second Mate on the Makawao. He continued as second officer on other ships of the Matson fleet, the alliteratively-named Makua, Maunawili, and Monterey.

On March 8, 1933, the U.S. Department of Commerce issued HBF's first Master's license, good for the customary five years, "to master steam and motor vessels of any gross tonnage, upon the waters of any ocean, plus first-class pilot, Honolulu, Hilo, Kahului."

He would renew this license periodically and add pilotage certifications during most of his remaining adult life. [3]

---

[3] By 1973, his first-class pilot certifications included San Francisco Bay and its tributaries to Crockett, San Pedro Bay and Los Angeles Harbor; Puget Sound between Angeles Point, Seattle and Tacoma via main ship channels; also harbors of Honolulu, Hilo, Kahului, Port Allen and Nawiliwili, Hawai'i.

Now it was time to look up close and personal at the oceans he had mastered.

Chapter Three: Heroic Feats

"EVEN A WINDLASS is better than no lass"--1933

The same month that he acquired his first Master's license, HBF took a surprising leave of absence from Matson. Why leave a job for which the 30-year-old, clearly on his way up, was well credentialed?

His decision may have been prompted by a failed shipboard romance. My evidence for this is the photo of HBF and his friend, George Grunewald, nattily attired in their gold-buttoned officers' uniforms, leaning against the Matsonia's windlass. On the back of the photo Dad wrote: "Even a windlass is better than no lass."

JANET GAYNOR (at right}, with a friend. Gaynor was one of the celebrities who toured the South Seas during the 1930s on Matson's elegant passenger liners such as the Monterey

Girls or no, heroic feats--winning tournaments, early inventions, first paintings noticed by critics years before their creators are recognized--seem essential to mastery. For a sailor, a long voyage by small boat--Dad was to make two--is equivalent to Picasso's first collages or Hemingway's *Big Two-Hearted River*.

Also, the restless HBF was becoming bored with the passenger ships. He'd been with Matson eight years since 1925, surviving shipboard romances, glamorous celebrities, grumpy shipmates and captains, and quantities of booze.

As he told the story to numerous reporters over the years, while serving as Second Mate on the Monterey in 1932 as she docked in Suva, Fiji, he fell in love with the Nomad, a 50-foot ketch that had been abandoned there by Howard Pease, a writer of boys' adventure stories. Dad tracked Pease down in Los Angeles, bought the boat (for $1,972), and invited three friends to make the 5, 561-mile voyage from Suva to San Francisco. What with side excursions to a dozen islands, vagrant winds, swimming, fishing and hunting, the trip covered more than 7,000 miles. (See Map No. 1, page 113.)

In early March, 1933, the *San Francisco Chronicle* reported:[4]

> Two prominent yachtsmen of the bay district sailed yesterday for Suva aboard the liner Monterey to assist in dispatching the yacht Nomad from the island to these shores.
> George Bray of San Francisco and Louis Durkee of Berkeley accompanied H.B. Ferris, new owner of the Nomad, who has relinquished his post as second officer of the Monterey. Ferris has appointed himself master of his floating property.[5]

Bray was a robust, easy-going guy who affected a monocle when talking with junior high students after the voyage. Lew Durkee, tall and reserved, was a hapless soul, accident-prone, who drowned in the Oakland estuary some years later in an unrelated boat accident. Rob Wright, the son of a judge, grew up on one of Fiji's outer islands, was a fine cook and fluent translator, who spoke many dialects of all the islands they were to visit. He was to become one of the South Pacific's most notable photographers.

---

[4] Newspaper clipping in possession of the author

After buying the Nomad in 1932, HBF only viewed her when the Monterey called at Suva every four weeks. During that time, he had her overhauled. Her masts were stepped (fixed in new blocks); nearly a thousand square feet of new canvas sails were cut. He planned to leave Suva, the capital of Fiji, after the hurricane season was finished around the end of March.

Lew Durkee, HBF, George Bray, on the Monterey, before beginning the Nomad voyage in 1933

HBF, Bray, and Durkee arrived at Suva in a tropical drizzle that continued for more than ten days. They took temporary quarters ashore while they scraped and painted Nomad. They replaced the unworkable galley stove with three Primus burners and a small portable oven, which served their cooking needs for the next six months.

Bow to stern, Nomad measured a few inches under 50 feet, with her water-line measurement two feet less. With a 13.6-

foot beam and 7.6-foot draft, she was a double-ender. Below decks, she slept four.

HBF observed: "The chief attraction of the engine room was one of the dirtiest and most dependable pieces of machinery that ever splashed oil in one's eye, a 16 H.P. Frisco Standard engine. The auxiliary equipment was a 2.5 KW lighting plant, a bank of 25 Edison batteries, a large motor generator for a radio set which we did not have, and the motor and coils for the ice refrigeration plant."

Mounted near the Nomad's ribs were two 250-gallon gasoline tanks, plus water tanks holding 300 gallons, half their water stores. They stored more water under two bunks in an aft cabin and more under the galley. They also took on new water whenever they found potable supplies during the trip. They stored canned goods in locker space leading from the aft cabin up under the cockpit.

While they were working, continual rain soaked them and their clothing. George Bright, Chief of the Suva Fire Department, allowed them to use the firehouse as shore headquarters, and to dine with the firefighters.

One evening when they had enough dry clothes, HBF and Bray dropped what seemed to be sufficient chain and heavy anchors to hold a battleship, left Durkee aboard, and went to a dance. That night Nomad went adrift. They did not discover their loss until the next morning, April 1, when at first they were positive someone had played an April Fool's joke on them.

HBF found the Nomad had drifted six miles across the Suva harbor. He rowed the dinghy toward it until his arms ached. Lew Durkee had hoisted a white towel--an ineffective distress signal--in the rigging. "We heaved our fouled anchors aboard and returned to our mooring of the previous night," reported the Ferris who was becoming a Captain. As another aspect of mastery, he was learning how to take full responsibility for his ship and crew.

After ten days of rain and bad weather at Suva, Nomad departed April 3, 1933. Shortly before sailing, Durkee caught his foot in the anchor line and became disabled with a dislocated ankle. They didn't discover the extent of his injury until they were outside the harbor. My guess is, they were so ticked at him that they would have left if he were dying.

The effect of Durkee's injury was mitigated when Rob Wright, a young Suva man, decided to come along at the last minute. Wright, whose daughter told me he couldn't afford a camera at the time, proved himself indispensable.

"Much of the future hospitality and courtesy that we were to enjoy on the islands where no English was spoken, we must attribute to Rob's fluent Fijiian," HBF observed.

The structure of the crew soon became clear: HBF, master; Wright, chief mate; Bray, chief engineer; Durkee, steward.

HBF's log indicated that their first night was the most hectic of the whole trip, because the sailors were not yet sure of what their boat could do. Their hopes of making a passage to the northeast of Suva vanished around midnight, when winds forced them to stand off to the southwest and to run for shelter near the southeasternmost point of Kandavu Island.

Daylight found the wind holding from the east and the sea still rough. Since the wind was sending in heavy seas, their only possible course was to the south. By afternoon Durkee's foot had swollen to immense proportions. It became imperative to find shelter where the foot could be taken care of, or at least rested.

By the second night, peaks of Kandavu to the north had disappeared and they had made no headway toward the island. With a rising wind, they came about and headed north, after which they took in the mainsail, trimmed the jibstay and mizzen, lashed the wheel, and went to bed.

In the morning they could see the peaks of Kandavu again. They found themselves headed up the southeast coast of that island toward Nglea Harbor, which HBF thought would shield them from almost any weather. However, they needed to spend some time searching for an entrance, hard to find from the deck of a small boat, because 13 miles of reef stretched ahead with only two small passages through.

Noted HBF: "It was late afternoon when we dropped our anchors behind Nglea Island, in as snug a little harbor as one would wish for. From our anchorage we were separated from the mainland of Kandavu Island by a mile of water. From this position we watched the sun impale itself on the high peaks of the main island before sliding from view."

For their first dinner in two days, they ate a 16-pound walu caught on the way in through the reefs. Afterwards, under a full moon, he and Rob rowed the dinghy to the Kandavu shore. HBF slipped a .38 calibre Colt automatic into his pocket for protection, but by the evening's end knew he would not need it. He left it back on the boat for the rest of the voyage.

When he and Rob landed on the beach, several natives carried the dinghy above the high-water mark. Others beckoned the two men into the largest native hut, where a fire of coconut husks smoldered and unfamiliar cooking smells greeted their nostrils.

Harold and Rob squatted on thick pandanus mats while three girls seated cross-legged on the floor chanted the rhythm of the various dances. In the background were the young men of the koro (village), some beating time on a hollow-log drum, others making good harmony. Still farther in the shadows of the kerosene lantern footlights was the kava preparation.

HBF's log called the drink, kava, "non-intoxicating," but scientific reports label it a powerful narcotic. He described its preparation, whereby kava roots are cut into small pieces, diced, and pounded into pulp, after which it is placed in a large wooden kava bowl and diluted with water. A long fiber hank is used to stir the mixture as well as to gather the sediment from the liquor. After it has been worked around in the kava bowl, this fiber mop is squeezed and the sediment shaken out.

He also described how the kava was served:

One of the girls who had been furnishing the entertainment up to this time, brought the coconut bowl of kava forward, offering it from her two hands extended, while on her knees. Before taking the bowl, it is customary to clap the hands twice. Then, after the girl has crawled back a few paces, one is supposed to down the bowl's contents in one gulp to the beat of three hand-claps from the donor. Then if you are a real diplomat, you smack your lips and say "venaca," meaning 'very good,' as you toss the coconut bowl back in the direction from which it came. The party lasts as long as the guests stay, and while it lasts there is kava, singing and dancing.

Morning brought an outrigger canoe full of coconuts alongside Nomad. Bananas soon followed, along with squash and green vegetables such as cucumbers. The sailors learned from the natives that no doctors were available; fortunately Durkee's foot had taken a turn for the better. A flock of wild ducks flew close, so the men shot three. In the jungle on Nglea Island, they tried climbing coconut trees. However, all save Rob proved to have deficient hands and feet for the job.

That afternoon Rob, George, and HBF made an expedition to the native village store, where a plug of tobacco, two buckets, and a few articles of clothing made up the greater part of the stock. They bought the entire stock of buckets and a garment apiece, which they called a "sulu." Then they started for the public bath.

Finding a cool stream gurgling over the rocks as it made its way from the cloud-shrouded peaks to the nearby sea, the trio used a big hole in the rocks as a bathtub. Like sailors everywhere, they brought all the dirty clothes they could find. The native women washed them some twenty yards downstream, within sight of the splashing and dipping.

In the evening there was another party ashore for the Nomad's nomads. After a repetition of the preceding evening's songs and chants, the natives called for a "taralala." All the village men sat around chanting while the newcomers stepped around over the pandanus mats with the girls. None of the native men took active part in the jig, but kept up an incessant rhythm of song and chant.

HBF explained:

> In doing the "taralala," or Fijiian foxtrot, the couples hold hands and face the same direction. The steps are two forward and one backward, but as foolish as it may seem, it was difficult for as poor a dancer as myself to catch on. George picked up the shuffle readily, soon adding a bolder step. He pepped it all up with a Highland Fling and threw in a bit of Black Bottom, which made a great hit with the natives.

The next days provided unparalleled fishing, exploring, and terror one evening because, when they moored a few hundred feet offshore, the wind came up, forcing them to spend the night only a stone's throw from crashing breakers. For two hours, they attempted to carry a second anchor out in the dinghy. During the process, the dinghy turned over twice before they could place the anchor reliably.

BARE-BREASTED beauties
of Ongea Levu. "Natives aboard
for inspection, about 75 of 'em,"
HBF noted in his log.

Soon they found two islands not on their original itinerary: Ongea Noriti and Ongea Levu, or big and little Ongea. These were notable because the shoreline overhung the water by 40 feet. The visitors found they could walk along under the shade of the beach for a mile at a time, being comfortable under the heat of mid-day. HBF attributed the structure to volcanic action on the atolls' coral reefs.

The travellers explored Ongea Levu for five days. The snow-white sand of its lagoon floors reflected myriad shades of blue and green. The islets and rocks inside the atoll took bizarre shapes: a turtle, a turkey, a pig.

They hunted rubee, a wild pigeon, attended another dance, and expressed relief when the natives ran out of kava. As you can see from the National Geographic-type photograph, HBF appreciated the native ladies. He did not write about whatever he may or may not have experienced, Perhaps my mother cleaned up his observations when she typed his log two years afterwards. Or maybe the native ladies thought too much of themselves to befriend the rambunctious sailors.

Good Friday fell during their stay, so they decided to see how a Fijiian church service was conducted. The natives found an enclosed bench for the visitors; everyone else sat on the floor.

While the congregation sang hymns of, as HBF put it, "familiar tunes and unfamiliar tongue," an accompanist beat on a large triangle. One bearded patriarch, Tomasi, raised his face toward Heaven and "groaned out" a 15-minute prayer.

Afterwards, Tomasi invited them to his house to eat baked taro, fish roasted in banana leaves, tea, and coconut pudding.

When they returned to the boat they found Durkee sitting near the entrance, gun in hand, in case the natives were dangerous. Weaponless himself, this seemed silly to HBF.

The night before they planned to leave, as they were starting back to Nomad, an outrigger canoe under sail slipped by them and up to the village at Ongea Levu. Tomasi shouted for them to return.

Back in the village, they found the canoe that had passed them. It held Tomasi's aged father and two brothers. The men had sailed up from Vatea Island, 50 miles to the south, in the craft, which HBF described as "so flimsy that I would hesitate to trust myself with it in New York Harbor on a calm day."

They had made the trip without compass or chart. Tomasi's brother related that they had started from Vatea a week before. After running three days out of sight of land and depleting their supplies of water and food, they had turned back again to Vatea, then resumed their journey to Ongea Levu. This second time, they made the trip in 15 hours with very light winds.

When Tomasi hinted that he would like to go to Vatea Island, the Nomad included that in their voyage. One senses from the log entries that HBF and his crew were delighted to be finished with schedule and "must-was."

Tomasi's father, the village leader back in Vatea, stayed on Ongea when the others sailed late one afternoon. The Nomad had Tomasi aboard, along with his wife and small son, plus a deckload of chickens, cats, carved wooden calabashes for mixing food, taro, coconuts, and bananas. The sailors were given part of the load. The remainder was a gift for the natives of Vatea.

Shortly after midnight a day later, a fair breeze put them abeam the reef at Vatea, a cigar-shaped island surrounded by an outlying reef. The only passage through this reef, on the northwest side of the island, caused HBF some hesitation, because his pilot book stated there was no entrance for anything more than a skiff.

However, following Tomasi's advice, they piloted through the snake-like channel entirely under sail. Before they rounded the last point, they could hear the beat of the tapa-cloth makers and the cry of "sail ho" coming from the village.

"As many of the villagers as could find canoes came out to greet us. When they found we had Tomasi aboard there was wild excitement," HBF noted.

Later they went ashore to find that Tomasi had assumed his father's position and hut, the largest in the village, at Vatea. The village treated the newcomers with songs and dances. HBF reported "superior" entertainment with familiar melodies such as "Old Black Joe" sung in native words.

Ptomaine poisoning prevailed on Vatea due to a run of spoiled fish. The day following arrival the Nomad's crew opened up a clinic. They found that almost every child in the village had sores, which they attributed to "none-too-clean" living conditions. For victims of ptomaine poisoning, they used all their calomel, castor oil, and salts. For the sores, they delighted the children by painting them with mercurochrome.

After five days, they set out for Vavau, but slack winds and the need to conserve fuel kept them at sea for several days. All one night, they lay on deck watching the volcano on Tofua Island light up the sky at intervals.

Morning found them near the illusive Falcon Island, of which HBF wrote: "The charts will show this as Falcon Shoals, for in 1926 a survey party found 13 fathoms of water where this island now stands out: 400 feet by 3.5 miles long, a huge pile of pumice and cinders. Nor has this recent rising been Falcon's only display of temperament; in the last 200 years it has risen or disappeared a half dozen times."

HBF wrote this in 1933. Falcon still is playing now-you-see-me, now-you-don't, as recently as 2012.

On the way to Vavau, winds forced them into a side trip to Nukualofa, the capital of the Tonga Archipelago, on Tongatabu. This diversion provided them with the most spectacular sight of the trip, the Tongan Monuments, described by HBF as "stone evidence of a tribe of diligent workers of the eleventh century."

The men discovered that Nokualofa was in mourning for a Princess, whom HBF described as a "sister" of Queen Salote, but who probably was one of her daughters. It was still raining. The black-clad natives were bundled up in fiber mats. The Royal Vaini, or palace, was closed to all visitors.

However, in the local club (read "bar"), HBF and his crew met two Britishers, "Messrs. Denny and Scott," retirees from the Tongan government, who offered to conduct them on the 27-mile trip to see the antiquities.

Setting out by motor truck, they saw the Lagoon of Olaki, where Captain James Cook first landed in 1773. HBF's new pals pointed out "the very rock that Cook first put foot on, and the tree to which he tied his longboat."

Coming to the village of Mua, on the site of the old Lapaha or King's Village, their hosts explained that because this was the center of the Tongan government and culture, and the dwelling place of the Tui Tongas (Tongan Kings) from the early sixteenth to the mid-nineteenth centuries, they would find some 50 structures. However, they suggested that the Nomad sailors would best spend their remaining time viewing the Langi Paepaeotelea, or platform of Telea, felt to be the finest example of Tongan construction and stone work. and the resting place of royal bones since the sixteenth century.

The Langi structure was 92 feet by 135 feet by 8.5 feet. HBF estimated the stones must have weighed between five and 20 tons.

Bumping and skidding over 18 miles of deep mud, stopping frequently to drink cool beer, the group next viewed the trilithon[6] structure, Haamonga, near the village of Kolonga.

Smaller than the Langis, also built in the eleventh century, the Haamonga Monument consisted of three gigantic coral limestone members, two upright, with the third a lintel

---

[6] *A megalithic structure comprising two large vertical stones supporting a third stone set horizontally, of which the most famous is at Stonehenge. Another is part of the Temple of Jupiter at Baalbek, Lebanon.

piece forming a huge arch. This lintel was tightly morticed into the tops of the upright members, and was not plumb.

Their hosts explained that the King, Tuiatui, ordered its construction to symbolize the harmony and brotherly love that he wished his two sons to observe after his death. The larger of the two uprights represented the elder son, the smaller the younger son, and the cross member the bond of common parentage.

The uprights were estimated to weigh 40 tons, the crosspiece 20 tons. The whole structure was named "Haamongamaui" in honor of the "Tongan Hercules, Maui."

Down a footpath, the travelers came to the shoreside remains of the royal city, Kolonga, where they picnicked, tidied up their site, and returned to Nomad with a load of Tongan mail to carry to Pago Pago for the anticipated arrival of the Monterey.

Several days later, driven the wrong way by northerly winds, the Nomad lay becalmed, abeam of Falcon Island for the second time. During the afternoon they saw the volcano Tofua giving off an occasional belch of smoke. Beside Tofua rose the cone of Kao, a 3,000-foot peak. After sunset, for most of the night, they watched Tofua send a glow heavenward every few minutes.

With a change of wind the next day, they entered the walled Vavau harbor shortly before midnight. The following afternoon, they sailed down the harbor to sea caves. From the dinghy, they explored a grotto where blue waters reflected upon stalactites that looked like a giant pipe organ.

From their anchorage in Vavau, they explored the high shores for several days before heading to Pago Pago, where they loaded stores, unloaded mail, and complained about high moorage charges. They took Durkee to the hospital, after which he "went missing" and did not appear in the ship's log again until they arrived at the island that HBF loved most: Puka Puka.

In my Orcas Island home is a quilt given to HBF when he left Puka Puka. As an only child reared thousands of miles north on Orcas, I've wondered if I could be related to anybody from HBF's voyages. If he begat other children anywhere, I would most like to have them been conceived and reared on Puka Puka, because the gentle way of life there must have produced lovely human beings.

Soon after the Nomad's lookout signaled the tops of the coconut palms on Puka Puka, also known as Danger Island, dozens of canoes came to greet the newcomers. In one was Geoffrey Henry, the native Resident Agent of the Cook Islands Administration, who directed others to carry an anchor onto the reef. This, with a hundred fathoms of line, held the Nomad for the next eight days.

The anchor had to be carried onto the reef because at Puka Puka there was no entrance to the inner lagoon. Even the native canoes required portage across the high spots in the reef. In order to keep Nomad headed off f the reef, they brought the anchor line aboard over the stern. Several native boys helped them stand watches to be certain the boat remained off the reef.

When HBF and Rob went ashore at dark to use the bathhouse, they were immediately surrounded by curious natives. On the way they had to shake hands with almost every adult male inhabitant of the island, and needed to repeat this process every time they came ashore.

HBF found the island "communistic in the best sense of the word." The population, a little over 600, was divided equally into three villages situated on the northernmost island. The southerly islands, reserved for copra, were only visited during the copra-making season, when the entire population of the three villages moved there. From Henry, he learned that when the copra was sold, the money was divided equally among the population. The youngest and the oldest received like shares. Proceeds were distributed through heads of families.

Population of the three villages were maintained through inter-adoption. "The head of a family has no objection to adopting an extra child, as he gets a greater amount of money for his household to compensate for the addition," HBF noted.

During the Nomad's stay, each village was assigned a day to send food aboard. George Bray and Rob Wright, each adopted by a village, participated in Puka Puka's annual two-day fishing contest, in which 150 contestants in 60 participating canoes used handwoven lines to catch bonita with live bait.

In the villages, the North Americans relished the fact that there were no regular hours for sleeping or meals. HBF observed that the native men rose from their night's sleep when the sun shone through the windows, but they built their windows on the west side of their houses so that dawn would not interfere with a good night's rest.

The Resident Agent, Mr. Henry, and his wife entrusted the Nomad's captain and crew with their son, Tonga, when they sailed June 1 for the 425-mile leg of their voyage to Penrhyn Island. They would leave the boy there to go on to Raratonga on another vessel. With sadness, they saw the last of Puka Puka, "that low coconut-covered bit of paradise."

What wind they had was driving them south, so they decided to look at Suvarov Island, an atoll lying 13 degrees, 17 minutes South and 163 degrees, six minutes West. "It was a long way off our course, but time and place had long since ceased to be important," recorded the beguiled HBF.

They found the trader's quarters in ruins on Suvarov. However, a large cement cistern furnished good water which they loaded up over the next five days. Bare-handed, they captured small rock cod and mullet, salting down about 50 pounds.

The Nomad spent many more days battling headwinds or sitting in calm weather; they swam overboard every day. On one 24-hour run they only made seven miles. Finally they caught a moderate southerly breeze that gave them better than 100 miles a day toward Penrhyn, the most remote and northerly of the 15 atolls that comprise its group.

Nearly a month out of Puka Puka, on June 29, they sighted Omoku, the westernmost island of the Penrhyns. Here, they traded clothing and cigarettes with the natives for black pearls, and enjoyed exceptional western cooking. HBF developed a lifelong taste for ceviche in coconut sauce. Durkee, after drinking too much and "feeling his oats," asked a visiting dignitary to find him a woman for the night (he was rebuffed), the only recorded instance of licentiousness on the entire trip.

The five days on Penrhyn were a whirl of dining and drinking with local officials and aboard Capt. Viggo Rasmussen's schooner Tiare, which departed July 5 for Raratonga bearing the Nomad's young passenger, Tonga. "He spent the hours weeping as though he had lost his last friend," HBF observed.

Two days later, when the Nomad departed for Honolulu, the local minister brought his congregation to play and sing. As a final gift before the sailing, the natives brought a 40-pound roast pig, hot from the oven.

This last leg of the voyage proved their longest stretch at sea. Again, they met winds contrary to those expected from government reports. This forced them to cross the Equator 150 miles west of their planned crossing. Soon after that, however, the winds picked up and "Nomad at last seemed to sense that we wanted to get some place."

Anxious to reach familiar territory, they began to find the watches monotonous. They drank coconut milk from the diminishing stores in the dinghy. They tried to roll cigarettes from their lessening supply of black South Sea Trade Tobacco, a mixture of tarred hemp and shavings. They ate beans, fish, biscuits, and the fish they'd salted down at Penrhyn.

HBF made celestial observations every day. They began to catch flying fish. Rob Wright taught his friends to make the Fijiian wind call, "Thangi mai," to bring freshening of the Trades. It worked, on the twentieth night out.

HOMECOMING--
"Friends were waiting to take us
to breakfast. Before the day was
over we were booked solid for the
coming week"--HBF

At 9:30 PM on July 28, 1933, they arrived at Diamond Head Light. At the entrance to Honolulu Harbor, they anchored until the Harbor Master's launch came out in the morning and directed them to proceed to Pier 12.

On July 29, 1933, the Honolulu Star-Bulletin headlined:

UTOPIA FOUND IN SOUTH SEAS
Ideal Colony at Puka Puka
Reported by Quartet
Here on Nomad
BY RAY COLL

When Sir Thomas More conceived his model kingdom, "Utopia," some 400 years ago, he might well have been writing about Puka Puka, or Danger Island, in the South Seas, according to Captain Hal

Ferris, who brought his ketch-rigged yacht Nomad into port Saturday morning after a 7,000-mile cruise among the islands to the South.

An ideal communistic life exists at Puka Puka, according to Ferris, where all are on an equal footing and everything is shared alike.

"They even share their hospitality," he said. "When we arrived, we were entertained one day by one of the villages and the following days were passed along to other villages who did their share in looking after us."

SHOWERED WITH GIFTS

Captain Ferris said he or his men did not dare cast a favorable eye on any object because the natives would immediately insist it was [for them]. "If we happened to look up at a coconut in a tree towering over us, the first thing we knew a boy was aloft plucking it."

As a result of this fine generosity Captain Ferris and his companions had difficulty in leaving the Island without a "bride" for each one aboard. "It was really embarrassing," Captain Ferris declared.

The next morning, the Sunday Advertiser ran a three-column by eight-inch photo of the vessel, with inset photos of its four crew. HBF told of looking for a cache of opium, supposedly worth $1 million, on Penrhyn, but not finding it.

LINES OF WELL-WISHERS
gathered to greet the arrivals.

HONOLULU WAS A ROUND OF 'GOOD TIMES' for the ensuing nine days. Above, cavorting near Waikiki, HBF with Jane Turner Houghton Walker, (l) who would provide a San Francisco introduction to HBF's future bride.

The ensuing 34-day trip to San Francisco was anticlimactic. (With modern hulls, the elapsed times have plummeted. The 2009 TransPac record, Oahu to San Francisco, was five days, 14 hours, 36 minutes, 20 seconds.)

On the 29th day out of Honolulu, Capt. Ferris made his last celestial observation. By dead reckoning, he should have been near the Farallone Islands. But, he heard, the Farallones' foghorn did not display familiar characteristics. He'd noted that before on the Malolo's trial run off Nantucket. He was honing the intuitive instincts essential to mastery.

Suddenly the Farallone light loomed out of the fog. HBF held the Nomad off and set a new course for the San Francisco light vessel, 15 miles away. Later he discovered the light signal had changed in the preceding few months while he'd been away.

When the fog lifted, they powered the Nomad through the calm morning to the quarantine ground, where they dropped the anchor at daybreak.

A year after the Nomad's 169-day journey from Suva, he wrote: "My South Seas cruise was over. I was glad to return to civilization but often wished that I'd [spent more time] along the way. Nomad is at anchor in San Francisco Bay, but she seems restless. It won't be long before she will be underway again."

NOMAD AT REST off Angel Island, 1933

Chapter Four: Lust and Wanderlust

Soon after the Nomad arrived in San Francisco, HBF made the smartest move of his life: meeting and marrying my mother, Virginia. She had grown up on Orcas Island in northwest Washington, an area similar to the Maine islands he'd enjoyed a decade ago. Another asset: she played bridge well.

In Honolulu, HBF had renewed his acquaintance with Jane Turner, who had gone there to teach at Punahou. Armed with her strong recommendation, and the gift of a magnificent embroidered silk coat he'd purchased in Honolulu just in case, he wasted no time.

Virginia and Harold met in October. The *San Francisco Chronicle* reported the wedding, not in the Society section but in the Shipping pages:

> **HAL FERRIS HAS GONE AND DONE IT**
> That adventurous young sailor man, Hal B. Ferris, who got leave from the Matson Company to go toSuva and sail the ketch Nomad back here. . . has gone and got married.
> The bride was Miss Virginia Gibson of East Sound, Wash., and a graduate of the University of California. At present Mr. Ferris, formerly second officer of the Monterey, has a shoreside job compiling a new cable code book for the company.

The couple were married Nov. 17, 1933 in City Hall in San Francisco, with Virginia's room-mate, Burt Lowry, and Harold's former Monterey passenger, Molly Snell, as witnesses. Then the couple settled into a small apartment in Burlingame.

Virginia typed a long memo to the U.S. Hydrographic Office, to let them know exactly what was wrong with their weather charts. She also helped him by editing and typing his

*MISS VIRGINIA GIBSON, a stylish
University of California graduate who could
type.*

Nomad log, on paper recycled from the telephone company where she had a day job.

He completed the commercial code. Matson used it for 11 years, thanks to Virginia's excellent typing skills and a good book on cryptography.

But no shoreside job could engage HBF for long. Within a year, the newlyweds put Nomad up for sale. HBF took a vacation, then another leave, from the family-friendly Matson.

CHOOSING THE RIGHT MATE--meaning someone you love--may be the most important part of mastery. Both Harold and Virginia, in this photo taken on their wedding day, look pleased with their choices.

He captained Nomad on a summer charter trip up the West Coast to Ketchikan. They sold the boat and returned to Orcas, where they went house-hunting.

Virginia showed total acceptance and understanding of the fact that nothing and nobody could keep HBF off the water for long. Soon, another voyage was to engage his attention for the next five months: November 5, 1934 to April 12, 1935. (See Map No. 2, page 114.)

This was a trip to Alaska--HBF's second of 1934--in mid-winter on the 33-foot yawl, Viking, together with a three-month stay in a cabin south of Wrangell. Three important differences between the Nomad's voyages and the new adventure: first, HBF started as a guest but, in his words, "the guest became the captain and the owners became the crew"; second, the weather was lousy, a far cry from the sunny South Pacific; third, during most of that time Virginia, back on Orcas, was pregnant with me. She didn't discover her condition until HBF had been gone for a month.

From that voyage, HBF would gain his enduring friend, Wayne Johnson, who served as his purser during World War II, and whose son HBF would mentor to another distinguished seagoing career.

In addition to Wayne, two other inexperienced young men were aboard the Viking: Dr. Jim Keenan and Charlie Adami. They declared themselves to be headed for the South Seas, although they lacked sailing and navigation skills. "Their reason for coming to East Sound was that Jim's family had a summer home there and they considered it a good place to do their washing before heading off to tropical climes," HBF recounted in a later article that Frank Evans later published in his newspaper, *The Orcas Islander.*

Another aspect of mastery: when you know a subject thoroughly, you need to teach it. Can't escape teaching it, in fact. During the week the quartet--Johnson, Keenan, Adami and Ferris--became acquainted, HBF taught the others the difference between a sheet and a halyard, convinced them that they should wait until April to start south, and that they might better take a short trip to Alaska via the Inside Passage.

From teaching his new greenhorns on this northern voyage, he would acquire expertise about weather, tides and currents, and whirlpools: an education that no ship could provide.

Leaving Virginia to hunt for a house, they left Eastsound November 5 for Juneau. Reasoning back from a newspaper story concerning the day they left, my parents must have celebrated the night beforehand, because I was born nine months later.

After mooring at one of the Vancouver Yacht Club's floats, they enjoyed sight-seeing and drinking for a few days before heading northwest toward Cape Mudge. Everybody developed colds, for which they used alcohol as medicine.

Running before a southeast gale, 100 miles north of Vancouver, all eyes searched for the Cape Mudge lighthouse through a dark night. The shores of Vancouver Island's east coast showed up occasionally, but they could not judge exact distances due to rain and wind.

Suddenly the light loomed out of the mist just as predicted. Then, in the inky dark, they saw a faint light in the windows of a Campbell River hotel. Looking for the hotel's dock, they went aground.

No cushy South Seas situation, this! Capt. Ferris noted quick actions by all hands:

> We unlashed the dinghy and prepared to run an anchor by which we had hopes of hauling off. However, the millrace around us would have prevented us from placing an anchor in an advantageous position even had not Viking settled hard before the anchors could be loaded into the dinghy. In the next three-quarters of an hour, Viking laid over on her port side with the masts elevated not more than 20 degrees above the horizon. At the end of an hour and a half we were walking around on the sand bank where Viking had chosen to rest for the night, with more moisture in the air than underfoot.
>
> It was questionable in my mind whether she would right herself on the incoming tide before the water started down the hatches. We made preparations accordingly. First, we carried two anchors and all our chain out toward the fast-receding water as far as they could go. After hooking them solidly in the rocks on that part of the beach, we made the chain fast to the heaviest piece of manila we had aboard, then

stretched this taut with our backstay tackle. We next moved everything that had any great weight to the high starboard side, nailed and caulked the afterdeck hatches, then crawled into the cabin. There, two of us slept on the floor braced against the port bunks, and two more slept against the outer port bulkhead, as the bunks were turned at such an angle that one would have needed to be glued in to stay in them.

We were all fully dressed and soaked to the skin. To add to our discomfort, it had been necessary to kill the stove fire while the vessel was resting at this angle. I had not intended to sleep, but I must have, for I started awake and climbed on deck to find Viking standing in an upright position and afloat. The dock we had headed for, the night before, was 150 yards to the south of us. We could not have missed it by more than 50 yards when we went by it.

The relieved sailors tied up the boat and trudged to the hotel for a good breakfast, hot baths, and a good night's sleep.

A new problem presented itself the next day: how to master Seymour Narrows, where Ripple Rock[7] lurked. A double-pronged mountain only nine feet underwater at low tide, its surrounding whirlpools had sucked in many lives. Captain George Vancouver called the area "one of the vilest stretches of water in the world."

Navigating the area safely, HBF knew, depended on arriving at Seymour Narrows before the tide began to change, creating the whirlpools. But, because the group dawdled over breakfast, they arrived a full hour later than the Captain had planned. Ripple Rock put on a display for them, as he recorded:

> Skirting the eastern bank of the passage to avoid the whirlpools, it was all the helmsman could do to keep any kind of course at all in the whirling rips that seemed to boil from the very bowels of the earth. Just

---

[7] Because it posed such a hazard to navigation, Ripple Rock was destroyed in 1958 by the world's largest non-nuclear planned explosion. Every time my family passed through the area in the Fifties and Sixties, HBF would marvel at this triumph of marine engineering.

abreast of the whirlpool we got a scare and a thrill which lasted for but a few seconds when one of the smaller eddies whirled our yawl 180 degrees off course against a full rudder. Before we had time to do anything about it, Viking's bowsprit had described a complete circle. For the next mile or so, our craft yawed like a drunken sailor. Indeed, I would have thought the helmsman drunk had I seen a ship steer such a crazy course in any other locality.

The incident served as a wake-up reminder to go strictly by the tide tables from then on.

Anchoring that afternoon at Knox Bay, some five miles past the northern end of Discovery Passage on the north side of Johnson Strait, they went ashore with shotguns and scored ducks for dinner later that night.

As they travelled up the Inside Passage to Alert Bay, on Cormorant Island, they noticed that the daylight hours were dwindling, and that the snow line along the mountains was lowering.

At Alert Bay, they visited the graveyard to look at the magnificent Kwakiutl[8] totem poles.

Starting off in another gale, against the advice of Alert Bay's police boat, they anchored late in the day in the Vancouver Island town of Hardy Bay. To dry their clothes and get some sleep, they rented rooms for two nights.

In addition to refining his understanding of tides and currents, HBF was learning where to find regular weather reports in this unfamiliar part of the world. At Bull Harbor on the northern tip of Vancouver Island, they met the two families who maintained the relay radio station.

The radio operator informed HBF that the full report of the weather for the British Columbia Coast was broadcast at 10 o'clock each night. He advised waiting for this report before starting across Queen Charlotte Sound, where 30 miles of open water lay before the next sheltered waters.

With a favorable 10 PM report, the sailors headed for Cape Calvert and the entrance to Fitzhugh Sound. The next morning, they moored near a river where they saw enormous flocks of geese. However, they couldn't get close enough to shoot them, so they had to content themselves with ducks. After several days, they steered north and west toward Milbanke Sound via Lama Passage.

Almost across the passage, the wind came up. They decided to look for a place called Newish Cove. As darkness fell, they found an entrance, but with a strong current against them. Cold and uncomfortable during the four-mile trek into the cove, their previous teamwork went out the porthole. As HBF told it:

> Wayne was at the tiller, while the other three were keeping a lookout forward. We got a sudden scare when a huge boulder loomed up about 15 feet ahead. We all shouted at the same time.
> I shouted, "Hard a-port."

---

[8] *Now pronounced and spelled KWAKWAKA'WAKW

> Charlie yelled, "There's a big rock ahead."
> Jim's warning was, "Put her over."
> Wayne inquired, "What did you say?" while keeping the helm amidships.
> By the time we had repeated our previous remarks, an eddy from around the rock swept us clear, even though Wayne did try to pull us up into it again.

They took soundings for two hours in Newish Cove but could find no bottom at the end of their 15-fathom lead line. So they ran into a small bight, used the dinghy to carry lines out to trees before and behind them, and settled in for the night.

Headwinds and rain slowed their progress for a few days. When they sailed into Butedale, a little cannery wharf and store on Princess Royal Island one morning, the town was brightly lit although only two families lived there. They said it was easier to leave the lights burning than to turn them off, as the current was generated by one of the nearby streams that plunged over a cliff into the deep waters of the Strait.

After buying more booze in Butedale, they shot a deer in the adjacent woods. The next day, they ate their first fresh meat in several days.

On Nov. 15, they journeyed overnight 115 miles to Prince Rupert, where they had, HBF reported, "a round of good times." It seems accurate to substitute "lots of liquor" for "good times." This particular bash lasted for two weeks.

Leaving Prince Rupert with hopes of a quick 80-mile trip to celebrate Thanksgiving in Ketchikan, they endured gales, rain, sleet, and injuries that almost meant they would not live to encounter any more holidays.

On the first day out of Prince Rupert, the Viking bucked a day of north winds, and sheltered that night in the Moffatt Islands. The next day, Thanksgiving, they caught a southerly breeze. As it was getting dark that afternoon, they were abeam Cape Fox when gale-force wind whipped out of the north, carrying rain and sleet. HBF noted the ensuing chaos:

Before we could get forward to take off the mainsail it was too late. As increasing gusts of wind laid Viking on her side, she would bring her head up into it and right herself up with sails luffing. This lasted for the next ten hours.

Solid water was pouring over our decks from fore to aft, a half-ton of it filling the supposedly self-bailing cockpit with each sea. I must have looked foolish, knee-deep in water, grasping the tiller, bailing with a tomato can. My bailing seemed to have good effects, for after four or five dips, the cockpit wold be cleared. Later, we discovered that the water was going down through the gearshift slot into the bilges. Charlie was working frantically at the pump in the cabin, thinking that a plank had surely gone off the bottom for such an amount of water to be there.

Jim was on the sick list, and was thrown out of his bunk. I found him on the deck of the main cabin amid all the pots and pans from the galley, books from the bookcase, and a couple of kerosene cans which had emptied their contents upon him. Not until the bilge pump fouled and the bilge water started to slop over the deck. . . could he get over his mal de mer.

Toward midnight we had our system of watches working more smoothly than the ship was running. Wayne and I relieved each other for 15-minute tricks at the wheel while Charlie and Jim fought the pump. We had all been soaked to the skin since early morning, so it was decided to break out the bottle of rum that was being saved for such an occasion in the medicine chest.

On my next trick, Wayne held the pot on the stove and made coffee that he lashed down, got out the bottle of rum, which he did not lash down but stuck behind the bunk, and came on deck to relieve me. With anticipation of something warm tickling my throat and sending its long rays through the frozen regions of my body, I went below with something near a smile on my face. Just as I went through the scuttle, Mr. 150 Proof Hudson Bay leapt from the bunk onto the engine block, smashed, and ran on through to the bilge. Life ebbed its lowest at that moment, but was followed by a quick succession of mishaps that gave us but a short minute to curse the luck on any one item.

Something had gone wrong with the jib, but in the blackness it was impossible to see what it was from the cockpit. I didn't relish the idea of going forward. [On doing so] I discovered that a halyard had carried away. I dragged the useless jib onto the bowsprit. Viking dived deep, and a brand-new supply of cold water covered me. The dinghy, which up to this time had been lashed bottom-side up on the afterdeck, decided to go wandering after a couple of seas had battered her.

The weather bureau at Ketchikan had registered a 40-mile blow while all of this had been going on, and our own barometer had gone from 29.78 to 29.03 between 5 o'clock in the evening and midnight. We hadn't been interested in either the barometer reading or the Ketchikan weather bureau, as we were out in it and had to make the best of it.

Around two or three in the morning, we passed the nadir of our wild night. It started to get better immediately after Jim realized there was a quart of 16-year-old prescription whiskey in his private medicine chest. Shortly thereafter, we ran up into the lea of Bald Island. When we again crossed the channel [to Ketchikan] it was almost calm, although the rain and sleet were still with us.

This may seem like revisionist history to some twenty-first century readers, but HBF's account was notable for its failure--characteristic of alcoholics--to notice their own impaired judgment. The Viking's captain knew where to obtain weather reports on his radio. If he had checked the 10 PM scheduled forecast before heading from Prince Rupert to Ketchikan, or, certainly from the Moffatt Islands, they could have stayed in port and avoided the mess.

Although HBF was to be credited with pulling himself and his friends out of the danger he'd gotten them into, alcohol was fast becoming his best friend and medicine of choice.

The mud flats at Ketchikan were white with the November 30 snow, the first of the year. After tying up at the public float and visiting the Custom House, they called a laundryman and loaded everything made of cloth into his truck

VIKING ARRIVES AT KETCHIKAN

for a thorough drying-out. They left the mess of debris inside the cabin behind a locked hatch while they made for the hotel.

Sailing from Ketchikan a couple of days later in a thick fog, they nearly collided with an airplane that was trying to find a place to take off. It brushed by them, not more than three feet away. Seaplanes weren't as common then as they are now, and the near-miss gave everybody a good scare.

A couple of days later, they sailed from Prince of Wales Island across Clarence Strait to the cannery wharf of a hamlet, Lake Bay. There they were greeted by HBF's "old friend, McKenzie McKinnon McDougall, aka 'Scotty,'" who invited them to share his cabin.

This turned into a four-month stay, although Dr. Jim Keenan by February decided he'd had enough and headed for Montana during one of the group's 35-mile treks to Wrangell for mail and supplies.

HAROLD FERRIS, WAYNE JOHNSON,
by the cabin at Lake Bay, with some of
the proceeds of their mink-trapping line.

They anchored Viking in the estuary leading to Lake Barnes. For daily expeditions into the surrounding country they used their own outboard motor and one of their host's boats, as their dinghy had been lost on the trip into Ketchikan.

Their first trip inland to Barnes Lake was half a mile back through a narrow estuary that could be negotiated by boat only at certain stages of the tides. There, HBF noted as much as 25-foot differences in tidal levels. The flood tide backed up into Barnes Lake and its adjacent lakes, but could not run fast enough to bring the lakes up to the sea level. Thereafter, halfway through the tidal cycle, rapids and waterfalls ran into the lakes. When the tide started through the estuaries, the sea level soon became lower than that of the lakes, so that the rapids and falls began again in the opposite direction. Of this phenomenon, HBF observed:

> Starting out with the tide running in our favor, we would make a speedy passage through the first rapids, and could cross the mile-and-a-half Barnes Lake in time to catch the first of the flood tide pushing on up through Dead Man's Lake and into Sweet Lake. After riding the rapids another two miles through Dead Man's, we'd come out into Sweet Lake, which is over five miles long and a mile and a half wide.

On one trip into Sweet Lake, they heard "a slapping and splashing that sounded as though a small navy was beating the waters with its oars." Shutting off the motor, they saw 25 swans taking to the air. Then a flock of 20 geese, spooked by the intruders, and much larger flocks of mallards, canvasbacks, and "butterballs" filled the skies.

The swans circled and landed a couple of miles away. Rowing toward the big birds, they saw several more wedges fly up and join the first group, until some 200 were together. When they flew away, they left one on the water. HBF and his mates were able to capture it because its wing had been damaged. Before freeing the swan they measured it: 98 inches from wing tip to wing tip.

That winter, they ate well: mallard duck, goose, fat clams at low tides, giant crabs, deer. "Life was . . . as easy as it is possible to live it," HBF commented.

With darkness complete at 4 PM, the men made dinner and did the dishes, after which they played cribbage while Jim read. Then HBF led a regular routine of study in course correction, dead reckoning, and celestial observation, after which Jim cooked a midnight snack. Wayne brewed beer out in back.

They also took over a six-mile mink trapping line for the other resident of Lake Bay, who left for a few months. It was a mild winter; they never saw more than a foot of snow. "As we dressed for the cold, we didn't mind the winter," HBF noted.

About the first of March they prepared to go further north, but a northerly gale delayed them for a week. Next, they sailed to Wrangell, then, through an all-day snowstorm, to St. Petersburg. Then they began the trek to Juneau, their original destination. En route the two-cylinder engine gave out, so they anchored one afternoon in Farragut Bay while Wayne and Charlie took the motor apart and substituted a piece of seizing wire for a spring in the timing gear.

That evening, just after rounding Cape Fanshaw, Charlie called his mates on deck to witness the aurora borealis, as they'd never seen it before. HBF observed: "The northern sky seemed lit up from 20 degrees above the horizon to the zenith. Shades of blue and purple flickered across the sky as though a huge searchlight was being played on waving curtains."

After an overnight in Taku Harbor, 20 miles below Juneau, they arrived in Alaska's capital at noon. They spent the next eight days with friends of Charlie and Wayne, sailing every day as there was always a good breeze.

Having had mostly fair winds coming to Juneau, HBF thought they were going to buck headwinds all the way back to Lake Bay. He was happy to be wrong. Leaving Gastineau Channel, which forms the eight-mile waterway between Juneau Harbor and Stephens Passage, they encountered winds that "seemed to come simultaneously from all points of the compass."

However, after crossing Taku Inlet, where a moderate gale was blowing off the glaciers, the wind turned and was over their stern the rest of the afternoon and night. The next afternoon, they pushed on through Wrangell Narrows, still holding a a favorable breeze and a good tide that put the Viking into Wrangell at daybreak. At noon they sailed from Wrangell to Lake Bay, traversing the 35 miles in six hours.

At Lake Bay they spent a few days cleaning up and loading gear aboard Viking. On March 31, 1935, they sailed for Ketchikan, with such favorable winds that they made the 70-mile trip in little over 24 hours. They stayed overnight, took on gas, and started south on what HBF hoped would be a non-stop passage back to Orcas Island.

They made this last leg in nine days and 19 hours, anchoring only twice. Once was to wait near Seymour Narrows for a favorable tide; the second was to avoid a snowstorm and thick fog.

When they were nearly home the old engine quit. Wayne and Charlie installed a new one before sailing, they hoped, for the South Seas.

More importantly for our family, HBF arrived home in 1935 to find his wife six months pregnant, and that he was a homeowner.

FIRST ORCAS HOME--The deed covered "Lots 23 and 24 of North Beach acre tracts. . . to be delivered within one week."

Through Virginia's careful finances--she hadn't been an economics major at Cal for nothing--she had plunked down $400 to H.B. Paige for the deed to their first home on Orcas. It lay on the east side of North Beach Road, a little south of what would be their long-term home.

HBF stayed home until I was born the following July. His personnel record indicates that he overstayed his Matson leave that year. It was not a good year for shipping anyway; crews were in conflict with the officers and power was shifting from the ship owners to the unions. HBF was never big on the unions, likely because he felt they diminished his authority

Though he was absent in 1934 and 1935, he and Virginia were living on money they'd saved from her Telephone Company job, his Matson earnings, and the sale of the Nomad. The boat disappeared from our family records after 1935, except for a brief news 1939 story to the effect that she was missing off the Oregon coast, with two youths aboard.

HBF now realized that he needed to return to sea in order to support his new family. In November, Virginia and their daughter moved to San Francisco for 18 months. She worked for the phone company while he rejoined Matson as second mate on the Mariposa, an 18,017-ton liner that carried passengers on the route among Honolulu, Pago Pago, Tahiti, Suva, Australia and New Zealand.

Coming off extended leaves, HBF needed to hustle for a few years to convince Matson that he was a serious candidate for top jobs and also to study for continuing licenses. As related in Chapter Three, he'd been awarded his overall master's license in 1933 before the Nomad voyage. However, all licenses needed renewal every five years and he added pilotage certifications during much of his career.

He worked as second relief mate also on the Manoa, Maliko, Manui, Maunalei, and as watch officer on the Malolo during the remainder of 1935. During 1936 he was relief officer on 13 separate ships, then served as First Officer of the Lurline in May, 1936. He was chief officer of the Matsonia for the next six months.

ALOHA HOUSE, 1937

HBF still loved going to sea, but with his new family he took paid leaves whenever he could. In January, 1937, he and

Virginia purchased the farm across North Beach Road from their first home. For $4,000, they acquired a house built as a tourist inn called "Aloha House," with a barn and pump house, on 80 acres. The purchase included an agreement to keep $3,000 insurance and to pay 1936 back taxes

Aloha House, 1937, had six bedrooms, two bathrooms a stone fireplace,and a huge basement to store all the wood George Kirchoff could deliver for its huge furnace. It required a 6 A.M. feeding by Mom on winter days. Built in 1905 for tourists from excursion boats docked in Eastsound, the house had an adjoining barn, well, and pump house. Since the 1970s, when Jim Klauder renamed it, it's been called Kangaroo House for Josie, the kangaroo HBF brought home from Australia in 1955. (See Chapter Seven.)

The Eastsound property soon included two cows, two goats, the first of many dogs, deer, and Mom's old horse, Lorna Doone. Eventually they acquired another horse, Chico, for me, along with plow horses named Huki Huki and Hana Hana (Hawaiian for "work work" and "pull pull"), pigs, (In a dispute

MOM HOLDS HER CHILDHOOD HORSE, LORNA DOONE, so I could ride her, in this 1937 photo

FARMER HAL home on leave, with Huki Huki and Hana Hana, the two plow horses purchased from Stan Englehartsen.

over whether she should purchase a manure spreader once, she named an old sow "Haroldene"), chickens, rabbits, goats, sheep, cats, dogs, and Josie, the kangaroo for which the present Kangaroo House is named. HBF brought home animals from ports around the world.

HBF teaching me how to ride my tricycle, and bottle-feeding a fawn

Mom saved Dad's allotment checks to buy adjoining land whenever she could. She and I milked cows together, but she did the bulk of the farm work, interspersed with frequent trips to meet Dad's ships wherever they docked. The Lavender boys, who lived a little way south on North Beach Road, helped with the chores when we needed to be away.

As Proverb 7.7 has it, iron sharpens iron and one person sharpens the wits of another. HBF's parenting often worked to sharpen and strengthen my rebellious nature.

Now in my late 70s, looking back on our conflicts, it's easy to see them as honing my own mind to make a modest writing career, marry an intelligent achiever, and to rear strong children. Mom and I also sharpened HBF's wits and perceptions; our lives whetted his interest in life.

We didn't always see the sharpening. The three-year-old me recalls being in a hotel room with HBF and my mother, when he was pretending to spank me. I didn't think that was funny. I grabbed a Coke bottle and hit him on the knee. He didn't think that was funny.

Nor did I appreciate his invention, in which I believed devoutly until the age of eleven (See Chapter Five), of a spanking machine that would pull a little girl in one end, spank her, and move her into a soundproof room until she quit crying.

HBF dealt with my mother's family, who were all over the place, by avoiding them, except for Sunday dinners and for those who played bridge. He used to sing: "Of all my wife's relations/I like myself the best."

OUR FAMILY LIFE may have been unusual, but for us it was uncomplicated. In this 1938 photo, above, the small dancing girl that was me is arriving with her parents for Sunday dinner with Great-Aunt Jean Donahue and her husband, Harry, at their farm just down the road from our new home.

Egos notwithstanding, we were becoming a supportive family. Dad's continuing mastery of his work and Mom's good economic initiatives seemed to prove that both parents had made excellent choices when they found each other.

Chapter Five: **The War Years**

The wind was kicking up whitecaps on East Sound as Mom, Dad, and the six-year-old me emerged from church. "Too windy to take the kayak out in the drainage ditch," said Dad, who was home on vacation from his ship. Mm agreed.

The cold brought with it a hint of early Christmas, with maybe a bicycle to replace my outgrown trike. However, my thoughts were more on spring because of the gift that old Mr. Akers handed me after the service. The gift was a soft, perfect hummingbird nest. Inside were two tiny eggs. Mr. Akers said he'd found it in the woods near his home in Olga.

"What happened to the hummingbird?" I wanted to know.

"Coon probably got her," Mr. Akers said.

"Did you thank Pete Akers?" Dad prompted.

"Thank you." I said, cradling the little nest in my hands.

Dad and I waited in our 1935 blue Chevrolet coupe, SJ-555, while Mom went into the store to pick up the *Sunday Seattle Times* for Great Aunt Jean Donahue. Her religious scruples prevented her from entering a commercial establishment on the Sabbath; she did enjoy reading the paper, however.

It was always the earliest edition, as it was printed on Saturday to be trucked 90 miles north to Orcas. So there was nothing extraordinary in the headlines from the Sunday paper.

Mom handed me the paper as she climbed into the front seat. I tucked up in back of them on the shelf where I read or slept on long trips such as the one we'd completed a few days before, to bring Dad home on a week's vacation from his ship, the Mauna Ala, in San Francisco.

Dad was driving north on North Beach Road toward our home when he turned on SJ-555's radio. As the news of the

Pearl Harbor attack shocked our ears, he pulled off to the side of the road. "Guess I'll be leaving sooner than we'd planned."

A few days later, we piled into SJ-555 again and headed for San Francisco. During the next few months we lived there, and at the Casa Madrona Hotel in Sausalito, while HBF completed classes on Treasure Island, received his commission as a Naval Reserve Lieutenant, and waited for his new ship to be built.

My seventh birthday, July 30, 1942, was scary. We drove Dad to Portland to ship out. His ship, the Joseph Lane, was to depart the Columbia River for San Francisco and the South Pacific. Japanese submarines were rumored to lurk near the mouth of the Columbia.

Our family never waited around to see a ship sail--that was supposed to be bad luck--so we drove away from the dock and Dad, to the first place Mom could find to park the car. Then she cried, the only time she allowed herself to do that openly.

Leaving the Columbia River that day, Dad would have seen the wreck of his former ship, the Mauna Ala, which had been the first merchant marine casualty of the war. Bound for Honolulu from Seattle with a load of Christmas trees when Pearl Harbor was attacked, she was ordered to turn into the river. All the lights were shut off so enemy vessels couldn't locate the area. While trying to negotiate the Columbia River Bar without lights, the Mauna Ala ran aground near Fort Stevens, scattering her cargo of Christmas trees over nearby shores.

I hung onto Mr. Akers' hummingbird nest for years; it represented a security that was being challenged for the adults, although they tried to hide it from me.

To put in context what happened next to my family and hundreds of thousands of others, the United States probably won World War II because of an accelerated shipbuilding program. It started with the 1936 Merchant Marine Act that created the U.S. Maritime Commission in order to modernize the merchant fleet.

During 1939-45, U.S. shipbuilders delivered some 50 million deadweight tons of large cargo carriers and tankers, and military vessels such as LSTs and aircraft carrier escorts. That comprised 5,601 vessels.[9]

In 1943 alone, shipyards built more tonnage than the total U.S. merchant fleet had been in 1929. The workhorse of the U.S. fleet was the Liberty ship, which accounted for 42 percent of this prodigious output.

NOUMEA, 1942-3

"Will we ever see such a shipbuilding program again? As unlikely as it seems, it is not impossible," Dr. Arthur Donovan, professor emeritus of humanities at the U.S. Merchant Marine Academy, wrote in his Preface to the 2001 edition of Frederic C. Lane's Ships for Victory, the authoritative history of shipbuilding during World War II.

However, during 1941 and 1942, shipping losses to the Axis powers exceeded new construction. Wrote Frederic Lane: "The perilous and feverish race between sinkings and construction was not definitely won until 1943." That, of course, was also due to improvements in radar that allowed ships to pinpoint submarines' locations. When the Joseph Lane slid down the Columbia River on my birthday in 1942, the 7,176-ton

---

[9] Lane, Frederic Chapin. *Ships for Victory: a history of shipbuilding under the U.S. Maritime Commission in World War II.* Baltimore: Johns Hopkins Press, 1951, 2001

Liberty began carrying materiél, with HBF as master, until mid-January, 1943. According to Hague Ports Database, her ports included San Francisco, LA, Wellington, Brisbane, Townsville, Port Moresby, Darwin, Thursday Island, Auckland, Antofagasta, Tocopilla, Balboa, and Seattle.

At Darwin, HBF saw the hulk of the Mauna Loa, the ship he had served as first mate in 1939-41 under one of his favorite captains, William O'Brien[10]. A Japanese bomber had sunk the ship on Feb. 19, 1942.[11]

HBF sent a diver down to wrest the ship's bell from the bridge. After the war, he brought the bell home to Orcas, where the author gave it to a resident, John Erly, in thanks for raising some of the funds for a new senior center in the early 1990s.

On January 18, 1943, HBF became master of the Mark Hopkins, a Liberty that had come off the ways at Marin Shipbuilding the previous day. She was 441' long, 56' wide, and could carry 2,840 jeeps, 440 tanks, or 230 million rounds of rifle ammunition. With a crew of 44 plus a dozen Naval armed guards, she was a true workhorse that served in the Pacific, European, and Mediterranean theatres.

K.K. Bechtel, president of Marin Shipbuilding, had to delay a banquet honoring HBF for a few months because the vessel immediately set off for the South Pacific, where Japanese Zeros menaced shipping.

---

[10] Ferris, Harold B. Continuous Discharge Book 050054, Department of Commerce.

[11] Worden, William L. *CARGOES: Matson's First Century in the Pacific*. Honolulu: University Press of Hawaii, 1981

It was a happy-to-be-alive HBF who took the microphone at the delayed Sausalito banquet, May 20, 1943, to tell stories and accept a plaque bearing the name of his ship from Mark Hopkins' daughter.

FORBIDDEN CITY, San Francisco, above: Wayne Johnson, Ruthie Brodin, HBF, Virginia, Bob Gilbert (Mark Hopkins officer), Louise Garbarini celebrated being alive during wartime; Below, HBF and Virginia at the Persian Room, Sir Francis Drake Hotel

BAL TABARIN PARTY with Georgina Templin Buck and her husband (left, top); Harold and Virginia (right, bottom).

After living it up in San Francisco night clubs, Harold and Wayne, his best friend and old sailing companion who served as Purser during all the Mark Hopkins voyages, traveled again to the dangerous ports around Australia, New Zealand, and other areas threatened by the Japanese. Somewhere between Sydney and Noumea, they rescued the captain and crew of the

MH De Young, 1943

M H De Young, torpedoed August 14, 1943 by a Japanese submarine.[12]

Three months later, when wartime news restrictions made it possible to tell the story, The Seattle Times[13] headlined:

---

[12] From Secret Log of the Mark Hopkins, Capt. Ferris's private enumeration of voyages from Mar. 13, 1943-Mar.15, 1945, in author's possession

[13] November 20, 1943

SEATTLE MAN'S HEROISM TOLD

Capt. Harold B. Ferris, Seattle mariner who sailed out of this port in ships of the Matson Navigation Company before the war, had a major role in a drama of the sea recently in the South Pacific, the War Shipping Administration said today.

Captain Ferris was master of the Liberty ship Mark Hopkins, which rescued the crew of the Liberty ship M.H. De Young, torpedoed by a Jap submarine. The De Young did not sink, but the attack left her dead in the water, the Associated Press reported. The tanker Quebec towed the De Young to an island. Under the direction of Captain Ferris the Hopkins, in addition to taking the De Young's crew aboard, also loaded her cargo. Capt. William Munda of Taylorsville, N.C., was master of the De Young.

The two Liberty ships bear the names of two pioneer Californians who were intense rivals in the early days of that state. The De Young was christened for the founder of The San Francisco Chronicle and the Hopkins honors the memory of the California capitalist who was one of the builders of the Central Pacific Railroad.

Captain Ferris was mate in the freighters Mauna Ala and Makiki and other Matson Line ships plying between Seattle and Hawaii before the war. He has a farm home at Eastsound, Orcas Island, in the San Juans, noted for its peat moss.

By the time the story appeared, the Captain and Purser had said goodbye to their sweethearts in Long Beach and were on Mark Hopkins Voyage 3--Oct.21-1943 to April 16, 1944--to Hobart, Tasmania, India, Ceylon, Aden, Suez, Alexandria, and, by April 16, 1944, to Savannah, Georgia.

Instead of going through the Panama Canal , they took the long route, through the Suez Canal.

SAYING GOODBYE--Harold and Virginia, Wayne and Esther Stockton Johnson in a Long Beach nightclub prior to leaving on Mark Hopkins Voyage 3, Oct. 21, 1943 to April 16, 1944, which would take them to Hobart, Tasmania, India, Ceylon, Aden, Suez, Egypt, and to Savannah, Georgia.

By the end of Voyage 4[14], from Charleston, S.C. part-way around the world and back to New York --April 29, 1944-March 15, 1945, she had traveled 75,352 miles.[15]

Much of the mileage must have been routine, as the Mark Hopkins made no less than 23 round trips back and forth across the English Channel after D-Day, ferrying officers, enlisted men, and cargo including U.S. Mail, to such positions as the beach heads of Utah, and Omaha, mainly from Southampton.

---

[14] Per the Captain's Secret Log, in author's possession

[15] Ibid, [Log not numbered, but New York is the last detailed page]

OFF FOX GREEN, part of General Patton's tank crew (HBF in middle front) The Mark Hopkins ferried troops across the English Channel to France and returned to Southampton.

'D DAY +3'--HBF caption of photo (above) that Wayne took from the port rail of the Mark Hopkins. The ship was not in the official list of ships at Normandy on June 6, 1944, D Day. However, HBF's Secret Log shows that the ship's main contribution went on for months afterward: 23 round trips ferrying troops from Southampton across the English Channel to France. Below, HBF riding a camel during the Egyptian part of Voyage 3

To relieve boredom, they photographed soldiers, entertained dignitaries, such as the Lord and Lady Mayor of Stretford, England, and developed earlier photos such as one of HBF riding a camel in Egypt, where he and Wayne toured the pyramids. Cribbage and bridge helped relieve the tensions. So did Scotch, inexpensive aboard ship.

For years, the man HBF mentored and I puzzled over a series of photos, mostly taken by Wayne, of the two merchant mariners with the Lord and Lady Mayor of Stretford, England. How, we wondered, did they become acquainted with such

A FEW DAYS AFTER D-DAY, HBF and Wayne entertained Frederick Cawley, the Lord Mayor of Stretford, England, and the Lady Mayoress, aboard ship. Wayne particularly enjoyed making elaborate menus, reminiscent of pre-war luxury liners.

personages and their aide, who carried the mace that symbolized high office?

For answers, we were given such yarns as that when they arrived in Stretford, they got drunk and were thrown in jail, and it took the Lord Mayor himself to get them out. Or, another possibility for us to ponder: British Customs tried to arrest them for giving free cigarettes to Britishers alongside the dock but HBF and Wayne told Customs that the Lord Mayor and his Lady were dining aboard. Outranked, the Customs folks backed off.

It wasn't until we looked at the written date on one of the photos--July 10, 1944--that we realized they must have been celebrating D-Day.

After the six-month Voyage 3, Mom and I travelled across country by train to meet Dad in Savannah and to visit in Charleston, Atlanta, and Washington, D.C. Then we hunkered down on Orcas for Voyage 4, tending the farm and developing compulsive habits of going to the Post Office in hopes of mail.

Soon after the war ended, the *Orcas Islander*'s lead headline[16] proclaimed:

CAPT. FERRIS LANDS BOYS IN INVASION
Home on Leave, Islander Tells of Invasion by Allied Armies

Capt. Harold Ferris, small boat sailor, amateur photographer of distinction and master of a Liberty ship that did its part in putting the Allied forces ashore on the Normandy beaches last summer, is home for a well-earned rest, after two years of constant duty. At his delightful home on North Beach, near Eastsound, he is relaxing, making prints from the many negatives he has made during his voyages to practically every part of the globe, and enjoying the companionship of his wife and little daughter.

Capt. Ferris had a short leave two years ago, but this is his first real vacation in four years. When he left Orcas Island in 1943 after a few days' visit it was to take command of the Liberty ship Mark Hopkins in San Francisco. His first trip in her was to the South Pacific and since then he has completely encircled the globe . . .

"She is a staunch ship," he says, "for not once did her engines stop at sea and she was in service every day in two years. What is more, there are hundreds of sister ships that have equally good records. Liberty ships may not be as fancy as the pre-war liners, but they are a lot better than most of the cargo boats of 10 years ago and they will do good service after the war."

After the Mark Hopkins had spent almost a year in many voyages that included in their ports of call such diverse places as Sidney, Australia; Karachi,
India; Aden, Arabia; and London, England, she found herself a part of that vast armada that put Gen. Eisenhower's armies ashore in France. She carried over many thousands of troops, 500 at a trip.

---

[16] April 26, 1945

Capt. Ferris grows a little awed when he recalls that operation. "No one would have believed it possible that such a great force could be moved with such precision," he says. "But it was done, and without doubt it is the most marvellous military operation in all history. Enough credit cannot be given to the men who planned it nor to the men who went ashore on those narrow beaches backed with sheer cliffs that bristled throughout every rod with machine guns, artillery emplacements and Europe's best fighting men. But they did get ashore and did take these fortifications with losses far smaller than anyone had any reason to hope for. I sincerely believe that our fighting men are the best and most efficient that the world has ever known."

After the allies moved into Belgium and took the port of Antwerp, the Mark Hopkins began to carry supplies there. Often as she plowed her way up the Scheldt the boom of artillery to the north was clearly audible, as the Allied and German armies battled for the Netherlands plains. And along much of the route the plains were flooded where the Germans had broken the dykes and let the sea in. Mile after mile of what had been fertile farms, orchards and populous villages were submerged, sometimes with only the tops of the houses above water. It will take many years to restore the productivity of these lands and the Hollanders are naturally pretty bitter about it.

Capt. Ferris was in Antwerp only a couple of weeks after the Allies had taken it, and says that the harbor works were in pretty good condition, considering circumstances, and quite capable of handling a lot of freight. The city was not badly damaged. He found the Belgians that he met friendly and he has great respect for them.

Asked about the boys who are serving in the merchant marine, as many island boys are, he said: "They are getting fine training and will develop into good seamen in a remarkably short time. I hope that after the war our merchant marine will be maintained and that all who want to follow the sea as a profession will have the opportunity. In the meantime, their parents and friends can be sure that they are being well treated, well fed and prepared for a career. Since the U-boat menace has been diminished to almost nothing, the merchant marine service is no longer hazardous; but at one time it was more dangerous than any of the fighting services."

Capt. Ferris was granted a 63-day leave, at the expiration of which he has been promised the command of a bigger and faster ship than the good old Mark Hopkins. He expects to spend most of his time ashore at his Orcas Island home. And he is going to be asked with insistence for the story of the 15,000-mile voyage that he made in the 50-foot Nomad, which he bought in Fiji and sailed clear to Alaska, with many detours and stop-overs. It's a classic of the seas.

After the initial joy of greeting Dad's return from war, I became disenchanted with the man for a time. First, he and my mother seemed to go into a world of their own that did not include me. It took growing up to understand that.

Second, the abundant Scotch that HBF had consumed during the war, and the cases he brought home and drank, did not make for good parenting. Indeed, subsequent events led me to think he may have had Post-Traumatic Stress Disorder. (See Chapter Nine) After one living-room episode where he was alternately angry and teary, the ten-year-old me ran down to the basement, grabbed a couple of bottles, and smashed them on the concrete floor.

Oddly enough, that action didn't produce a spanking. He was never physically violent with my mother or me. Both of them agreed I deserved a spanking for smashing the bottles. Gravely, he led me into the kitchen for that to occur. He held a finger to his lips for silence, then directed me to Mom's rag bag and indicated I should stuff the soft cloths into the back of my jeans.

Then he whispered, "Yell!"

Recognizing a good conspiracy, I complied. As he made loud hitting sounds, I shrieked. I doubt that my mother was fooled.

"Don't worry," he told me. "Alcoholism always skips a generation. My grandfather was an alcoholic. It completely missed my father. So it'll miss you too."

I accepted that for many years until I had children of my own. I wouldn't wish alcoholism on my own progeny. Nor, I suspect, did he. Better, it seemed, was to adopt different directions than over-drinking.

Sixty-eight years later, my discovery of HBF's main World War II log occurred during a search for something entirely different: recipes that Dad sent to *Sunset Magazine* for their *Chefs of the West* feature. (They used a couple of them and sent him a chef's hat and apron as reward.)

For years, I've stacked old books, many saved for my grandchildren, in an unpainted, falling-apart armoire in the garage. I wasn't even able to unlock one side of it. But while searching for the *Sunset* recipes I found a pry and pried open the locked side.

Inside was a small tan lined book. On its cover HBF had printed, in red ink: 'Secret Log of the SS Mark Hopkins.' All ship's masters were required to keep Secret Logs in addition to their Official Logs. They were probably supposed to turn them in after the war, but he never did, thank God!

So I started typing up the contents, which on the surface were mind-numbing categories such as latitudes, longitudes, fuel and water consumption, distances traveled (mostly back and forth across the English Channel in Voyage 4), dozens of ports, average speeds, how many U.S. Army officers, men, and jeeps were aboard.

However, a significant fact emerged from HBF's patient enumerations: one little ship, a Liberty weighing 7,194 tons, traveled nearly 100,000 miles during the war, from Australia across the Indian Ocean, Ceylon, India, Gulf of Aden, Red Sea, Suez, Egypt, the Mediterranean, the Atlantic, England, took soldiers to Positions Utah and Omaha in France, helped to supply troops up through Antwerp and the Netherlands, back to New York.

Aboard, Dad and Wayne played bridge and cribbage, honed their photography skills, drank too much Scotch, and

RETURNING FROM NORMANDY several weeks after the first invasion. Note the gun emplacements on Mark Hopkins' bow and sides. Many years after HBF kept his Secret Log, reading it made his daughter grateful for this evidence of patient work.

managed to avoid getting killed in the Pacific by Japanese Zeros or submarines, or in the Atlantic, North Africa, and around England by their German counterparts.

Chapter Six: Post-War Aviation

To set post-war flying in context, planes have landed on Orcas since the 1930s. Chuck Holmes landed several times in Lester and Zoa Cowden's Crow Valley field in the 40s. But it wasn't until Edgar Kaiser landed his DC-3 in the Ferris hayfields near Eastsound in the spring of 1946 that anybody began to see the location as a potential airport.

Only returned veterans had seen planes as large as the DC3. Its wheels ground into the muddy hayfield so that the pilot could not turn it around. A tractor towed the airplane backwards toward the dike on the north end of the marsh, so that it could take off.

THIS GLEAMING DC-6 belonged to shipbuilder Edgar Kaiser, who had recently bought a home in Deer Harbor.

HBF was fascinated; his ship Joseph Lane had been built in the Kaiser shipyards at Portland. Carlyn Kaiser, with whom I attended summer camp at Four Winds on Orcas for two years in the 1940s, had been the flower girl at the ship's launching. It is not recorded whether Edgar Kaiser paid a landing fee, but my parents agreed that such fees could be a future source of income.

ORCAS ISLAND AIRPORT, 1946

Before the first fly-in, in 1946, Harold Jensen and Harold Boyer bulldozed the initial runway, about a third of a mile. Ray Pinneo built two hangars and an office. We bought a roller to drag behind our new Case tractor. I learned to drive it to tamp down the runway, which slanted uphill a few hundred feet from its southern end.

At left, above: Harold Boyer and Harold Jensen helped carve out the runway with Jensen's TD-9 bulldozer. At right: Ray Pinneo built the hangars and office in 1946.

Dad learned to fly from Bob Asplund, in an Aeronca Chief (NC23973), in which he soloed June 27, 1947. Bob Schoen, who had been flying since the FAA lifted wartime civilian flying restrictions, obtained his commercial license in July that summer.

As with everything else HBF did, his involvement with flying was inextricably mixed up with his ships. His motivation was clear: he had a ship moored in Seattle since September, 1946. The Rensselaer Victory had been sold to the Dutch, who took their time about picking it up. As the ship's master, his main responsibility was to board the vessel once a week to be sure the chief engineer had turned over the engines.

Photo courtesy of Mary Schoen

FIRST FLY-IN AT ORCAS ISLAND AIRPORT--A dozen planes, more than anyone had seen at one time, graced our hayfields in 1946. These included an AT-6, a Taylorcraft, and at least one Seabee. At the fly-in, HBF showed off the new roller that, we hoped, would keep the north section of the runway from sinking into the peat bog on which it was built.

His first solo cross-country flight, necessary to obtain his private pilot's license, was July 8, 1947, notable because the engine failed on the Aeronca Chief and he returned to Boeing Field. Undaunted, he soon was flying to the Rensselaer Victory, landing on the dock beside the ship, boarding long enough to be sure she was operable, then flying back home to Orcas.

NEW KID ON THE DOCK--HBF starts the prop on the Aeronca Chief that allowed him to fly from Orcas, land on the Seattle dock next to his ship, make sure it was okay, and return home in a single afternoon. No more waiting for ferries!

By the end of September, 1947, HBF became Captain of the Matson ship J.T. McMillan, on runs to India and Korea, which meant he no longer needed to land on the Seattle docks. When it was geographically handy and the FAA (later CAA) wasn't too nosy, he landed on a Portland dock to visit Wayne and Esther Johnson, who were raising their family in Eugene.

HBF LANDED ON A PORTLAND DOCK, above, when one of his other commands, the SS Sonoma, was tied up here. (Photo courtesy of Capt. Robert Johnson)

In October, 1947, my mother began keeping the account book for our Orcas Island Airport[17], which by then had a gas tank, two hangars, and an office that boasted a real Coca Cola machine. Bob Schoen, the Union Oil Company dealer, supplied the gas, which we resold to pilots. He also rented, either a monthly tie-down or hangar space, for $15 a month, for the Eastsound activity of his new airline, which became the first commercial air service on the West Coast: Orcas Island Air Service.[18]

An energetic entrepreneur, Bob decided to incorporate his airline during the winter of 1947. He ran a contest to name the fledgling. Carol Clark won a free round trip to Bellingham, a $7 value in those days, for her name: Island Sky Ferries. Early in 1948, her suggested name replaced "Orcas Island Air Service".

Around 1950, Bob's Union Oil dealership became too busy for him to focus any longer on his airline, so he sold Island Sky Ferries to a Portland doctor, Wallace Haworth. His son,

---

[17] Her account book, covering 1947-53 and Island Sky Ferries 1951-53, is in the author's possession. She and HBF sold the airport to the county in 1958. (See Chapter Nine)

[18] R.E.G. Davies and T.E.Oursler. *Commercial Airlines of the United States.* Smithsonian institution Press, 1965. P. 300.

Dave, sold it to HBF and Virginia in 1951. They hired Roy Franklin, who had flown for Bob and the Haworths, to fly the main routes between Eastsound, Waldron, Friday Harbor and Bellingham, with occasional charters to Seattle, and extra money for teaching students, including me, how to fly.[19] Roy first showed up in Mom's account books in May, 1951, with an April salary of $291.50, plus a percentage of fares.

In December, 1948, Matson appointed HBF Master of what would become his favorite ship, the Sierra, a cargo-passenger vessel which, before it was re-named, he had commanded as the Sea Centaur when it was built in 1945.[20]

He captained the Sierra for the next five years until August, 1953. (See Chapter Eight) He enjoyed the route and bridge-playing pals Down Under, including Capt. Harold Ruegg and his family in Sydney. The latter was in charge of the Cook Island Dependencies for several years.

During this time he was away for three months, then home for six weeks. The hiatus wasn't useful for maintaining his flying skills, although he did manage to fly occasionally in Australia. In 1951, he earned an Australian certificate to validate his U.S. Private Pilot license, so that he could pilot small planes Down Under.

As HBF's confidence grew, so did his daring. He liked to fly alongside the bridges of ferry boats and dip his wings at friends. He once landed the little Aeronca Chief in a Chehalis pasture, where he bent a wing strut.[21]

---

[19] My logbook showed 47 hours as a student pilot; I soloed the summer after completing high school. Mom logged 11 hours under tutelage by Bob Fawcett, but she did not solo.

[20] Matson bought the Sea Centaur and renamed her Sierra, the third of their ships to bear the latter name; she took cargo and passengers on the Down Under route that included Fiji, Samoa, Australia and New Zealand. Her sister ship, the Sonoma, was also a C-3.

[21] HBF's pilot logs, in author's possession

He enjoyed flying past the stone tower on Mount Constitution and swooping down its north slope, gleefully pointing out boats near the outlying island of Sucia to his terrified passengers. (Photo, end of chapter)

HBF was generous when anybody needed his flying skills. He was quick to fly Dick Burghardt to the hospital in Bellingham to have his broken wrist repaired, and did the same a few years later for Dick's sister, Patty, when a horse kicked her in the face.

Mary Schoen recalls that HBF brought a stuffed koala bear from Down Under to her son, John, who treasured it for decades. I still have the toy kangaroo Dad brought, before he brought home Josie, the live one (See Chapter Seven).

Before flying to Seattle, HBF often picked up a newspaper to drop to a family who lived on tiny Smith Island. If he was going to San Juan Island, or to Bellingham, he often picked up groceries to deposit on Orcas for anyone who'd run out of supplies.

Carol Clark recalls him leaving a bag at their door with the comment, "Can't stay. Off to Australia."

Mom and I managed the airport, which meant running down from our nearby house when a plane landed, to see if they wanted gas or a tie-down. We put out smudge pots at night as flares along the runway to guide pilots on emergency flights or for anyone who wanted to practice night landings. She also kept the account book for the airport and, by 1951, for Island Sky Ferries.

When I received a scholarship to an independent school in Tacoma in 1951, Mom had to do it all by herself, along with managing the farm and the variety of animals HBF kept bringing home. (See Chapter Seven)

In addition to Bob Schoen, some of the 1947 customers for gas, tiedowns, hangar rentals, or occasional taxi service to Eastsound, included: Silver Fliers (Seattle); the Orcas Aviation Club; Bob Hayden; Dr. McKenzie; "Zarbell, Burkhardt & Aeronca from Seattle;" "Coast Pacific;" "Duane Forks;

"Mainlock, Auburn;" "Bell, Yakima;" "Mt. Baker Flying Club, which included Sharp Bros., Bellingham;" a Dr. Meyers from Yakima; Mathews; Bloomquist; Burton C. Risser, Denver, Colorado; Ed Lavender, who took flying lessons; "Leigh, Redwood City"; Jack Haworth, 805 L St., Renton; Aviation Industries, Olympia (three planes for tie-downs); Galvin Air Service; Nelson, Sedro Wooley; and guests for such resorts as Ansel and Flo Eckman's Buckhorn Lodge.

Mom recorded 175 passengers during April, 1951, plus 86 pieces of freight ($5 each). Fares from Eastsound to Bellingham were $4, one-way; $7, round trip. From Friday Harbor to Bellingham passengers paid $5 one-way, $9 round trip. She noted $1,072.50 in fares during May, 1951, with an additional $113 from charters and $67.41 from freight. By June, fares were down to $1,008.50; charters were up a little, to $157; freight brought in $60.35.

By May, there were 307 passengers, and she recorded "cash & charges" of $1428.26, although she was soon to discover that people who charged didn't always pay their bills.

In June, 292 passengers flew Island Sky Ferries, mostly to Bellingham or Friday Harbor.

By July, 1951, there were 316 riders, bringing the four-month total to 1,070. A year later, July, 1952, saw 403 passengers, bringing the year's total to a whopping 4,828. By the end of October, that total had grown to 6,044.

However, by November, 1951, Mom stopped keeping detailed passenger records because she went Down Under with Dad on the Sierra for three months. Upon her return, she kept the books until they sold the air service to Roy Franklin and his father in 1953. He moved headquarters to Friday Harbor and re-named it San Juan Airlines.

Mom and Dad still maintained the airport, which attracted increasing numbers of private pilots and folks who liked to watch airplanes, and a few people who rented hangars.

Flying had other uses. Fred Nicol, who with his father was the premier contractor on Orcas after World War II, remembers toilet-papering the Sierra. Roy flew over the ship while Fred and Harold Jensen draped it, stem to stern, with several rolls of the white stuff, so that small boats could recognize the vessel and pick up the cases of Scotch.

Sophomorish? You bet! These guys had been through a major war; their objective was to have fun and catch up on whatever they'd missed.

A juicy evening for some Orcas Islanders it was. HBF dropped several cases of Scotch overboard in Boundary Passage near Saturna. A dozen small boats   picked them up. He undoubtedly had learned this trick during Prohibition on the old Malolo.

JIMMY SMITH AND HIS SISTERS--Their parents, Orville Smith and his wife, who built a home near Buckhorn Lodge, played bridge with Harold and Virginia, and flew in frequently. Both sisters were adopted; one became an accomplished jockey who married Fred Astaire.

COLLEGE FRIEND and the author pose in early Fifties on the "Green Hornet," the Dodge that Island Sky Ferries used to take passengers into Bellingham. Bob Schoen's earlier Orcas Island Air Service used a vehicle known as the Whippet.

In December, 1953, Fay B. Hall, who wrote the dot-dot-dot column for the *Orcas Islander*, noted: "Harold Ferris giving the natives a good scare with his moonlight plane rides. . ."

HBF gave our family a nightmarish ride on the last day of that year. His middle brother, my Uncle Frank, needed a haircut. Dora Cadden, the Orcas barber, had recently retired. So Dad offered to fly Frank over to Bellingham to have the Leopold Hotel clip his hair.

Dad wanted to pick up a bottle of Scotch because he had finished off the household supplies the preceding night. Mom wanted to get groceries at Safeway. She and Frank and our cocker spaniel, Foggy, climbed into the back seat of our four-place Stinson Station Wagon for the 12-minute trip. I hopped in front, in the co-pilot's seat, next to Dad.

Clouds towered to the east as Dad took off to the north on the little runway that we'd had built over the peat bog and hayfields on our farm.

Having soloed the preceding summer, this was a route I knew well, at least on a clear day. It was rapidly becoming evident that this was anything but a clear day.

As the altimeter rose to 1,500 feet, we banked to head east and soared over Parker's Reef. Ahead, the clouds over Lummi Island loomed densely. Looked like Bellingham might be getting some snow, or at least heavy rain.

"Nothing we can't go over," Dad said, pulling back on the wheel so that we rose to 4,000 feet. By the time we got to Lummi, we needed more altitude to clear those towering clouds. 5,000 feet. . . 6,000 feet. . .7,000. . . we kept climbing. By now we would have been over Bellingham Bay, which was obliterated by cloud cover. Bellingham Airport, off to the north, sported even higher clouds.

Dad banked to the north. Suddenly we were enveloped in clouds. He tried to turn back the way we'd come. Still more clouds.

"Airport's over there," he said. "Little more altitude and we'll go right on in."

Fifteen minutes later, it became clear that no matter how high we went, we weren't going to escape that merciless cloud bank. "Aren't the mountains off that way?" I started to ask, then realized that Dad didn't know any more than I did.

I started praying, feeling guilty because in a previous incident while flying home from Mexico[22] a few days earlier, I'd promised God that if we survived, I'd give up smoking. We'd survived; I hadn't quit. Maybe I didn't deserve to live, but surely our Maker would have pity on Mom, Dad, Frank and Foggy?

"Watch out!" Frank yelled from the back seat. "That dive was steep!"

I looked at the altimeter. It showed that we were still climbing.

---

[22] We'd spent my Christmas college vacation in Baja California. While returning, darkness set in. A Mexican Army soldier, stationed at the unlit Santa Rosalia Airport, saved our lives by using his cigarette lighter to ignite grass along the runway so we could see where to land.

"Frank, don't be a nervous Nellie. Nothing to worry about," Dad rasped.

I was learning that when a plane climbs and dives like that, the instruments always are a few seconds behind what's actually happening. Again, we climbed. Again, we dove. Over and over and over, maybe for 45 minutes. The plane shook like a dog emerging from a swim, and whined like a buzz saw cutting a log.

In addition to being disoriented, at least three of us were scared witless. Dad seemed unconcerned. "Watch for the ground," he cautioned me, "so we'll know whether we're over mountains or flat land."

That seemed reasonable. Ten minutes later, through a blessed hole in the clouds, I saw a hayfield about a thousand feet below.

"There's a hole. Looks like a hayfield!" I told him.

By way of reply, he dived down through the tiny opening. We came out about a hundred feet above land. . . but the clouds were closing in again.

"We're going in!" Dad shouted. He cut the engine. We drifted over a fence and started to touch down in that hayfield. Too late, we saw water glistening under the grass tops.

The Stinson touched, bucked, and turned over on its back. The prop buried itself in mud. My head banged into the steering wheel on my side. Foggy leapt from the back seat and cowered in my lap.

Suddenly there was silence, a welcome relief from the whining engine. I didn't care whether we were upside down or right side up, as long as we were on solid ground.

We all piled out of the plane. I held my nose, which was dripping blood. Frank had a suspicious yellow stain down the leg of his khakis. Dad was the first to speak.

"Frank," he said, "You didn't get that haircut but you certainly had a close shave."

Clipping from Belingham Herald, *January 1 1954*

HBF's pilot logbooks, covering the years he flew between April 14, 1947 and January 17, 1956, recorded 854 hours, 20 minutes of flying time. Unlike his meticulous Secret Log of the Mark Hopkins, the later pilotage entries were often sloppy. The last flight he recorded was January 16, 1956, to "Alt Field," which was probably Ault Field on Whidbey.

He noted being "weathered in" at "Alt". The next day, he landed in an outlying field, citing "out of gas."

He was only 53 years old when he quit flying, clear proof that alcohol and aviation do not mix.

He would still accomplish a notable maritime success (Chapter Eight) A notable failure still lay ahead (Chapter Nine), plus years where he regained some control over his worst enemy.

Chapter Seven: Organs, Centaurs, Kangaroos, Cocker Spaniels, & Other Four-Footed Friends

Centaurs, kangaroos, cocker spaniels, and organs--the musical kind, rather than the body parts--all jumble together in my aging brain. This is because HBF's favorite ship, the Sierra, originally was built in 1945 as the Sea Centaur. She carried some of his most notable four-footed friends and his organ.

SEA CENTAUR'S CENTAUR--by the Mississippi artist Robert Oliver Crofton III, was a 9x12-foot oil painting. Re-named the Sierra in 1947, the C-3-type ship carried freight--11,000 tons compared to 7,000 tons for the old Liberties--and 12 passengers to Down Under ports.

Matson flew Dad back to Philadelphia to pick up the Sea Centaur, which resulted in a family reunion and the decision that the middle brother, Frank, would move from Washington, D.C. to Orcas with my grandmother, Evelyn.

As the *Oxford Classical Dictionary* notes, the ancient Greeks thought centaurs represented wild life, animal desires and barbarism. They were lustful and overly fond of wine.[23] Bulfinch[24] describes them as having been fully admitted to the company of man.

Although I have no reliable information about HBF's lusts, and he was fonder of Scotch than of wine, a centaur metaphor fits his human relations. Some animal lovers are, in my experience, introverts who don't like the company of people. HBF enjoyed both, and music as well

On the ship Alameda in 1953, he brought 22 wild camels, destined for motion picture companies, circuses, and zoos, from western Australia to Suva and Los Angeles. Two-month-old Henry, who, HBF reported to the Suva newspaper, "got his sea legs and did just fine," rode along with some ostriches.

---

[23] Oxford Classical Dictionary, 2nd Edition, 1970.

[24] Bulfinch, Thomas. Airmont Publishing Co.: New York, 11965 (ppr.)

"O, YE'LL TAK' THE HIGH ROAD"--Influenced by having seen Harry Lauder at the National Theatre while HBF was growing up in Washington, D.C., he loved entertaining humans or animals by playing his organ. "Loch Lomond" was his favorite.

Later, he brought Josie, who, according to HBF, became domesticated by listening to him playing the organ. The other members of the Ferris menagerie, including a pair of Royal Golden Cocker Spaniels, mostly ignored the little kangaroo, who soon grew to become a big kangaroo.

HBF and ROBERT JOHNSON, son of Dad's shipmate, patted Josie when she came from Australia in 1955.

HBF made the error of telling reporters that he planned to rear a colony of kangaroos on Orcas. The resulting flap made for a wonderful Seattle Times cartoon and story:

Seattle Times, April 27, 1955

BY GEORGE N. MEYERS

Josie, the pioneer kangaroo of Orcas Island, today languidly sniffed the domain where, in some imaginative minds, kangaroos one day may be catapulting from the landscape like popcorn, as far as the eye can see.

Josie sedately disembarked yesterday from the seagoing vessel of her master, Capt. H.B. Ferris, who hinted in Portland, Ore., a few days ago that this kangaroo might be the matriarch of a colony of her kind on Orcas.

Ferris said the next time he sails his freighter, the Alameda, to Australia, he plans to fetch a mate for Josie.

The merest inkling that the fauna of Washington might be augmented by displaced marsupials set officialdom to thumbing the wildlife by-laws.

No wild animal may be imported into the state without a permit," declared Burton Lauckhart, chief biologist for the State Game Department. "It would be illegal to release any wild animal to propagate."

Hesitantly, Lauckhart added: "I feel certain this applies to kangaroos. [They] are a little out of our line."

John R. Vanderzicht, state parks director, pondered the question of kangaroos multiplying at will on Orcas Island and making a trampoline out of the place.

"If they could be taught to hop around within the confines of Moran State Park and commit no nuisances, they could become a valuable tourist attraction," said Vanderzicht.

"But I'm afraid they would have to be fed. I just looked it up in the book. There is no provision of funds for feeding wildlife, kangaroos, or whatever."
Edward J. Johnson, director of the Woodland Park Zoo and an old kangaroo hand, concurred.

"Unless proper diet were provided, kangaroos certainly would raid gardens to get their vegetables," said Johnson. "Anyway, without shelter, kangaroos would catch cold and freeze their tails in winter weather.

"There really wouldn't be any worry about kangaroos crowding people off the island. A pair of kangaroos won't produce more than one joey a year."
A joey is a baby kangaroo.

"Moreover," Johnson added, "girl kangaroos are highly selective in their mating. They don't swoon for just any boy kangaroo that hops down the pike. It would take quite a while before the island could be said to be infested with kangaroos."

Orcas Islanders--small fry particularly--welcomed Josie amiably and with delight.

"I do not feel my life and property are endangered," said Thad McGlinn, operator of Templin's Store where islanders foregather to pass the time of day and render community decisions.

"If all kangaroos are as sweet as Josie, we say they'd make mighty fine neighbors."

In 1970, fifteen years after he and Virginia brought Josie home, HBF wrote about her[25]:

> We were in Adelaide, South Australia, when a friend gave us this two-month-old kangaroo. In Australia a baby kangaroo is called a "joey," so this being a female, the name "Josie" dropped upon her with very little thought from her foster parents: my wife who was traveling with me, and myself, the ship's master.
>
> Chips, the ship's carpenter, built her a large pen adjacent to my quarters, a space usually reserved for passengers; sunbathing and recreation. It was going to be another month before I'd be picking up States-bound passengers in Brisbane, so Josie moved right into a first-class billet.
>
> Josie was a very frightened twenty pounds of fluff. She continually licked her forelegs, probably because she didn't know how to bite her fingernails. It is a trait of frightened kangaroos to lick their forelegs.
>
> For a few days it appeared as though it would be hopeless to expect that she would be domesticated. Then one day when I was playing my electric organ, we noticed she had her nose and front feet pressed against the screen door to my quarters. Later we left the door open when the organ played. She hopped over the high door sill, came right up to my organ bench, and looked up.
>
> From that time on, she ate rolled oats out of our hands and stopped licking her forearms except when strangers tried to get too familiar.
>
> By the time we reached Brisbane, where we boarded our twelve home-bound passengers, the pen had been dismantled and Josie had the run of the ship.

---

[25] Unpublished essay, edited by the author

She could even make it up and down the companionways between the upper and lower decks.

It was two months by the time Josie had her first look at the U.S.A., in Los Angeles. In the meantime she had become the darling of all aboard. When she hopped up to a person, she would look up as though she were asking a question. It got to the point where passengers and crew were quoting "what Josie had said a few minutes ago."

Besides having Josie aboard, we had Auckie, a Royal Golden Cocker Spaniel that I'd carried with me aboard ship since she was five weeks old. Auckie would have nothing to do with Josie; her nose was out of joint on account of this newcomer.

Arriving in Los Angeles, we found Pier 168 empty of freight, to the great delight of Josie, who could cover the 600 feet of dock and back in an incredibly short period. She was most happy to be on solid ground again.

Across the street from our Pier was a long grassy strip. I thought it would be nice to have Josie smell some American grass. So, with one leash on Josie and one on Auckie, we crossed the street. About the time that we got on the grassy strip, I realized I'd made a grave mistake.

Traffic was coming to a screaming halt; fenders were attacking fenders; motorists were vowing mayhem on motorists who had stopped to have a quick look without giving benefit of signals.

I hurried my charges safely back aboard ship, where they stayed until we arrived in the next port. That morning, we found a secluded little park. Josie was enjoying the grass, hopping merrily around while Auckie lay beside us, surveying her rival with jaundiced eyes.

Suddenly, at the far end of the park, two large dogs entered and made for Josie.

Auckie, realizing that there must be solidarity in every family, got her hackles up and drove the errant hounds from the park before they could molest Josie. But she still didn't like the Australian monstrosity.

[Back home on Orcas] we were surprised to discover how much survival instinct this Southern Hemisphere animal brought with her. When a rain squall was imminent, she could be found on dry ground under a bushy cedar tree, the likes of which she couldn't possibly have known in her native land even if she'd been there a lifetime, instead of a bare eight weeks.

From the time she arrived on Orcas, Josie was never penned up or tied. She was always just about where we expected to find her when we looked. On a sunny day she would find a declivity in the back yard, where she planted her rear end with one of her great legs protruding skyward. Then with her forelegs she would preen the fur on the big leg and seem to admire it. I used to say that it reminded me of a chorus girl taking a bath until my wife wanted to know where I'd seen a chorus girl taking a bath.

One day Josie was several hundred yards from the house when, out of the woods, a three-pronged buck deer appeared. It jumped sideways. So did Josie. For 15 minutes they danced back and forth, about 50 paces apart. Josie decided she'd seen enough; she made 30-foot leaps toward the house. The buck made a similar decision and ran back toward the woods.

Arriving at the house, Josie looked back. Finding that the buck was not chasing her, she returned to their original meeting ground. The buck returned for an encore to their original dance. After that Josie came home in leisurely fashion and we never knew her to look for a fast buck again.

Josie had most sensitive hearing. Whenever she started away from the house and we wished her to return, a few notes on my organ would stop her in her tracks. After a few bars, she would bound back onto the porch and peer through the door to get to the source of the sound.

Music, dancing, and night life proved to be her undoing. We never thought she left her cozy bed at night until around 3 AM one morning, a neighbor brought her home. There had been a dance at the Odd Fellows Hall, a mile and a half away. Evidently she was attracted by the music and went over to show the locals what a real hop was like. Around 2:30 AM she hit the middle of the dance floor. I understand that a great number of people took the pledge.

Abut a month after this incident, there was another dance at the same place. She was making for the hall when she was hit by a car. One of her great legs was broken. We flew her over to a vet on the mainland.

She didn't want anyone but my wife near her. She snuggled up to her much as a human child might have done, confiding her pain in short mews, the only sound a kangaroo can make.

The vet inserted a long, stainless steel internal splint parallel to the broken bone. For a few days it appeared we might save her. Her favorite food was Virginia's Martha Washington geraniums, which we'd kept out of her reach before. Now we picked them for her.

After two weeks she was moving around and even managing to get up, but not down, steps. Then the vet removed the internal splint. A few days later Josie died from an infection. Even Auckie seemed to join in mourning this little friend from the animal world who had become part of our family.

HBF TAUGHT DANIEL, our crow, to pull a cigarette out of a pack. Pusan, a Korean chow, learned to do a graceful, stretchy "Bow down." This cuddly pup and others served as bridges for our love during his absences.

Dad particularly enjoyed teaching animals. Auckie and Gibraltar, the golden cocker spaniel pups given to him by a harbor pilot in Auckland, were among the most teachable of all our family pets. I, myself, was a little jealous of Auckie when

HBF had her doing "square root," not my forte.

HBF's math trick was always a hit. "Auckie, what's the square root of nine?" he'd ask. "Arf, Arf, Arf," she would answer. He coached her up to proclaiming the root of 25.

DEEP-. WOOLED CORRIEDALE--On the back of this portrait, HBF wrote Mom from Australia: "This is what our ram looks like in the matter of wool quality. I have not named him and will leave that up to you and Janet. Something like 'Australian Prince of Orcas'? I think we have something that will go down in our family history as a better buy than Nomad. Love, H"

Somehow the sheep never qualified as pets. You couldn't teach them anything. None of the other farm animals liked them because they smelled bad. I can attest to this, having been assigned, in shearing season, to jump into long burlap bags full of the wool to compress it.

"This smells rotten," I'd complain.

"Think of it as lanolin. It's good for your skin," HBF would say.

In addition to bringing home pets while he was master of the Sierra, HBF experienced acupuncture for the first and only time. It was entirely successful.

As he told it, in 1954 he had a long-standing problem with his knee, probably the one I'd hit with a Coke bottle as a three-year-old. It "went out" periodically, with intense pain. While bringing the Sierra into the harbor at Papeete, Tahiti, he reached for a chart and fell flat on the deck.

After the ship was docked, he sat himself down to rest, with his knee propped up. Usually when it buckled, he had needed to remain immobile for a week or so.

The French Customs officer expressed sympathy and insisted that HBF see his "Practitioner." Dad said he feared that nothing short of surgery could make his knee usable.

The Customs officer insisted. HBF obtained a crutch from the ship's hospital. made it down the gangway, and into the officer's pickup truck. He put the crutch in back of the truck, and stopped by his office to get his bicycle and stow it also in the truck.

There were long lines in the practitioner's office. HBF soon noticed that even the small children showed no fear at having small golden needles stuck into their bodies.

When it was his turn, HBF had misgivings. The practitioner expressed surprise that HBF was unfamiliar with the treatment, which, he said, had been practiced by the Chinese for several thousand years with great success.

Within minutes, the Practitioner had inserted five needles into areas around HBF's knee and calf. When the Captain stood up, the pain was entirely gone. His savior would take no money, nor the box of cigars Dad later brought from the ship, He did accept one cigar.

Outside the office, HBF soon found the Customs pickup was gone, along with the crutch; the Customs official was so confident of recovery that he'd left his bicycle for Dad to ride back to the ship.

Eighteen years later, the pain and incapacity had not returned. In retirement, as we shall see in Chapter Ten, HBF weeded rows of garden on his hands and knees, jumped from dock to his boat, without recurrence.

In 1970, he returned to Papeete and tried, without success. to find the Practitioner who would only accept one cigar.

Chapter Eight: Saving A Ship

"We refine our memories until they are pure gold," the late Herb Caen used to say. One of HBF's most golden memories needed no refining. It was when he saved his ship, Sierra, caught in a violent 1951 storm.

The year following the Sierra incident, Noel McDonald described HBF well in his column of March 19, 1952 in the *Auckland Star*: "Harold B. Ferris, master of the American Matson Line freighter Sierra, is searching for the perfect life. Already he has had his fair share of adventure, seen most of the world . . . But he is not satisfied.

One of HBF's favorite sayings was "Never let the truth interfere with a good story." He described me, for instance, as having soloed at 14 (happened when I was 16) and supplied feature stories to well-known magazines, "This won her a $2,000 scholarship to one of America's famous finishing schools for girls." Mr. McDonald was undoubtedly influenced by HBF's affectionate hyperbole.

In retrospect, HBF and I expected perfection in each other. Inevitably, both of us were disappointed. However, his feat of saving the Sierra was a happy cause for celebration.

At my "famous finishing school," (where I have now celebrated my 60th year since graduation), on December 4, 1951, the headmistress called me before breakfast to announce that my father's ship was in trouble off the Oregon Coast, and that they would be offering prayers for my family in morning chapel. I was worried, because my mother, Auckie, and our car also were aboard the Sierra.

Our prayers must have worked, for by the next day the radio news indicated that the Sierra had crossed the Coos Bay bar safely and was at anchor inside the harbor. Other news stories followed.

COOS BAY TIMES account: "The seamanship of the captain, Harold Ferris, was praised by local waterfront observers."

In these, from Seattle, Portland, and Coos Bay, we learned that gale-force winds, more severe than had been predicted, had opened 7/8-thick cracks in deck and side plates. According to the Matson Company newsletter, MatsonNews,[26] HBF "slowed his ship down to three knots, just enough to maintain steerage way, although at times it was necessary to increase the speed and use full right or left rudder to bring the ship back on course whenever the head fell off more than 10 degrees while heading into the wind. .The sea was tossing the Sierra and her crew about like a cork."

---

[26] *MatsonNews*, January-February, 1952, P. 17.

HOWLING GALE opened seven-eighths-inch crack in deck, in 50-60 foot seas. It went all the way across the top deck and down the port side.

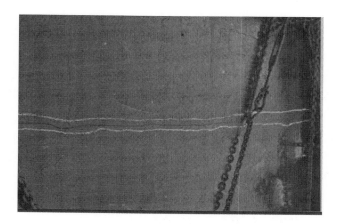

When it was safe for crew members to venture on deck without fear of being blown away, HBF directed them to rig 14 heavy chains to hold the plates together.

Acting as a prudent seaman, HBF turned his vessel into the waves' troughs to lessen the strain. The Sierra, now about 20 miles off the mouth of Coos Bay Harbor, wallowed, rolling 35 to 40 degrees to each side at ten-second intervals.

Although the bar pilots were unable to go out because the seas were running so heavily, Capt. Vernon Johnson of the Sierra's sister ship, Sonoma, which was in Coos Bay at the time, advised HBF by radio that his vessel could be brought safely across the bar.

"With split-second timing and full cooperation from the engine room gang, he held back until just the right sea came along, then calling for a surge of speed from his engines he rode in with the sea safely over the treacherous bar," MatsonNews reported.

Afterwards, the Sierra proceeded to a Portland shipyard, where the Albina Machine Works replaced six damaged hull plates.

Randolph Sevier, President of Matson, sent HBF a personal letter of congratulation "that your expert handling of the Sierra unquestionably prevented much more serious damage to the vessel than that which actually occurred."

The ship's master was a hero, to his family as well as to the maritime world.

Drawing by James Wilson

Chapter Nine: A Notable Failure

HBF was so successful at much of what he undertook that it would be easy, in this memoir, to overlook a notable failure. With the understanding of my later years, however, has come the ability to write about it.

Why did it happen? Take a man with a single passion: in HBF's case, the ocean. Make it impossible for him to pursue that passion, add the acquired habit of drinking too much alcohol, and you set the stage for an explosive situation.

The Hawaiian newspaper headlines of February, 1958[27], told the first part of what would become a horrific chain reaction.

On Feb. 10, 1958, HBF's ship hit an under-water pinnacle, 200 yards off Ninini Point, Kauai. The ship, the Hawaiian Craftsman, sustained more than $150,000 damage including two gashes in her No. 3 hold, with some oil leakage. Matson built log booms to contain the oil and keep Nawilliwilli Harbor from contamination, and the Craftsman was towed to drydock at Pearl Harbor.

Lois Stewart--a good family friend and Honolulu Advertiser columnist--went to bat for HBF. Right afterward, in her column, Air Lanes/Sea Lanes, she noted: "There was a great deal of sympathy along the waterfront yesterday for the Craftsman's skipper, a nice guy with a long and unblemished sea record."

In her next column on the subject, she noted that the U.S. Army Corps of Engineers would be asked to survey the area where the grounding had occurred. The Coast Guard said the Corps would be asked to do new soundings to see if there had been coral growth since the charts had been drawn.

---

[27] THE HONOLULU ADVERTISER (s), February, 1958

Cmdr. T.K. Whitelaw, the same man HBF had helped, back in 1927, to save the Malolo on her trial run when she was rammed by a Norwegian freighter, by now was the Coast Guard Marine Inspection officer. He said he would send divers down to see if a new pinnacle had been created since the charts were drawn. "If so, there's some blasting to be done," Stewart noted.

The survey showed not only new growth--a "massive underwater pinnacle" which the Craftsman had hit--but also outdated Coast and Geodetic Survey charts.

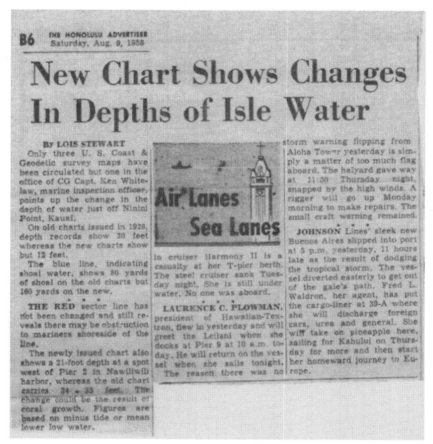

B6 THE HONOLULU ADVERTISER
Saturday, Aug. 9, 1958

New Chart Shows Changes In Depths of Isle Water

By LOIS STEWART

Only three U. S. Coast & Geodetic survey maps have been circulated but one in the office of CG Capt. Ken Whitelaw, marine inspection officer, points up the change in the depth of water just off Ninini Point, Kauai.

On old charts issued in 1928, depth records show 30 feet whereas the new charts show but 12 feet.

The blue line, indicating shoal water, shows 80 yards of shoal on the old charts but 160 yards on the new.

THE RED sector line has not been changed and still reveals there may be obstruction to mariners shoreside of the line.

The newly issued chart also shows a 21-foot depth at a spot west of Pier 2 in Nawiliwili harbor, whereas the old chart carries 34 - 35 feet. The change could be the result of coral growth. Figures are based on minus tide or mean lower low water.

In cruiser Harmony II is a casualty at her T-pier berth. The steel cruiser sank Tuesday night. She is still under water. No one was aboard.

LAURENCE C. PLOWMAN, president of Hawaiian-Textron, flew in yesterday and will greet the Leilani when she docks at Pier 9 at 10 a.m. today. He will return on the vessel when she sails tonight. The reason there was no

storm warning flipping from Aloha Tower yesterday is simply a matter of too much flag aboard. The halyard gave way at 11:30 Thursday night, snapped by the high winds. A rigger will go up Monday morning to make repairs. The small craft warning remained.

JOHNSON Lines' sleek new Buenos Aires slipped into port at 5 p.m. yesterday, 11 hours late as the result of dodging the tropical storm. The vessel diverted easterly to get out of the gale's path. Fred L. Waldron, her agent, has put the cargo-liner at 39-A where she will discharge foreign cars, urea and general. She will take on pineapple here, sailing for Kahului on Thursday for more and then start her homeward journey to Europe.

"On old charts issued in 1928," Stewart wrote, "depth records show 30 feet." In the Ninini Point area, current maps indicated a water depth of 40 feet and no coral heads. If the maps were inaccurate, the ship's master would not be as culpable as HBF appeared to be.

However, Matson didn't see it the same way. After the hearings, the company asked HBF to take a six-month leave of absence--unpaid--while the whole mess was being sorted out among insurance, Coast Guard, and company.[28]

That decision may have meant that Dad's record prior to Ninini Point was being questioned; Stewart's judgment of "unblemished" may not have been entirely accurate.

My mother told me of a prior accident. In that one, HBF had come in to a southern California port with a "snootful," had banged into one ship and caromed off another. In that ensuing Coast Guard hearing, he was asked how he would account for the collisions.

HBF was said to have replied: "Sir, it was just one of those days." He got off on that one.

More of "those days" had occurred for HBF and myself after the plane crash detailed in Chapter Six. After that one, in 1953, I probably suffered from concussion in addition to a broken nose. I stumbled through my college classes. Without knowing how to voice my anger, I disliked Dad for his alcoholic rants and for what seemed like constant criticism of me.

The following summer, 1954, I decided not to come home for vacation from college, much to HBF's anger and Mom's chagrin. But, at 19, it was a relief to be on my own. I dropped out of school for a year, obtained a proof-reading job on the newspaper in my college town, paid my own rent and groceries. After a year, I qualified for in-state tuition, which I paid until the end of my junior year.

Then, a little after the time of Josie the Kangaroo, we started speaking again; I still wasn't fond of HBF but it was good to see Mom again. When they offered to pay the tuition for my senior year at the University of Oregon, and invited me to come home for the summer afterwards, I accepted.

That summer of 1958, I walked into a maelstrom by comparison to which Seymour Narrows, pre-Ripple Rock destruction, would have been a millpond.

---

[28] Matson Navigation Company personnel record

The first indication I had that HBF was not entirely himself--his large alcohol consumption by this time was the norm--was when I came home unexpectedly to find him reading the diary I kept in my bedroom. As if this weren't provocative enough, he went to my mother and announced:

"Janet has become a Communist."

Although we were coming out of the McCarthy era by this time, HBF had used the fear that I might become a Communist in college to block my desired attendance at the school where both my mother and grandmother had graduated. That was a sore point. I reacted with fury to his announcement that his worst fears for me were realized.

I slapped him. Only later did I realize that my diary said nothing whatsoever about Communism.

That night, Mom told me that HBF was having a difficult time, because of the Matson suspension after the ship accident.

For the next few weeks, nothing special happened. Dad, Mom and I accompanied my new beau, a nephew of close family friends, to the Seattle Boat Show. He won the door prize, a week's cruise on a yacht. Since the beau didn't know much about navigation, Dad offered to captain the boat for a trip into British Columbia.

The trip, with Dad, my beau, his cousin, Mom and me, went well. We cruised the magnificent fjords going into Princess Louisa Inlet; we picked blackberries, fished, hiked, and swam in warm water gushing down the mountains from a glacier. I was beginning to like my friend, with whom I'd skied the previous winter. We may have held hands a couple of times, but with the lack of privacy on the yacht, it's unlikely that anything else occurred.

All thoughts of him went out the window, however, soon after we returned to Orcas, when I became reacquainted with a man about whom I'd read for years. His mother, a funny, accomplished writer whom I admired, had written extensively about her family. I'd met him before, the summer after high school. He was now in dental school, home for summer vacation. I was infatuated, and exceptionally happy when, after a few weeks, he asked me to marry him.

We figured it all out, without talking to my parents about it. We decided I'd find a newspaper job to help him finish dental school. I went to the nearby mainland to look for work, and was fortunate to be hired as a reporter on the *Bellingham Herald.* He completed his vacation with his folks at their island cabin.

After a few weeks, we decided it was time to tell my parents. I came back to Orcas, that fateful Saturday, and met my fiance at the ferry. When we arrived at the house, we were surprised to find several cars in the driveway, the house full of people.They were having a bridge party.

My new fiance found HBF on the back porch and said he wanted to marry me.

"I wouldn't count on it, fellow," HBF said. His nose was red, his face blotchy. "She was spooning with another guy last week."

While this had a grain of truth--our Princess Louisa cruise had been a month previously--this was embarrassing. A disheartened young couple, we hurried past the bridge-players as fast as possible and went to the Saturday-night dance at Deer Harbor.

These, on Orcas, were delightful occasions. Family members of all ages attended. The music was a mix of square dances, schottisches, and what became known as "slow dances."

When the dance hall closed, around midnight, we had a drink with friends, then headed back across the island. Then we parked at the beach, a half-mile from my house, and discussed what to do about my parent's earlier outburst, without coming to any conclusions. Then we hugged, kissed, and dozed for an hour or two.

About 3 AM, we decided to return to my house. Surely, I thought, Dad would be more sensible when he realized we were in love.

However, as we drove into the yard, we saw him standing on the front porch with a shotgun.

"Do you want to come to my parents' house for the night?" my sweetheart asked.

"No," I replied, "I can handle this."

He parked in front of the house. Then he came around the car to open my door. That's when HBF hit him. With the butt of the gun. My fiance fell to the ground, holding his face.

My mother appeared, grabbed the gun, and went inside the house to call the doctor and the airplane to fly us to the mainland hospital. I cursed HBF. Then I tried to comfort my bloody friend.

Our marriage plans soon were kaput. My unlucky fiance, after surgeries to repair fractured zygomatic bones, returned to dental school, graduated, married and had children.

By the time the criminal charge was filed, HBF's six-months' unpaid leave from Matson had ended. An undoubtedly-nervous HBF had gone back to work for his company.

Under the headline, "RETURN OF FERRIS," Lois Stewart wrote in her Honolulu Advertiser column in late August, 1958, "Biggest news along the waterfront among the many friends of Capt. Harold B. Ferris, is his scheduled return. . . next Monday morning.

"Ferris has been on "leave of absence" for six months after [his ship] ripped her bottom off Ninini Point, Kauai, last Feb. 10. He has spent the time at his island home in the Strait of Georgia off the Washington coast," concluded Lois, who at the time knew nothing of HBF's violent action nor, of course, of the court cases that would follow.

My former friend's family sued HBF, whose initial response to both civil and criminal charges was to hire the best-known legal firm in Seattle to defend him. He didn't want to settle the civil suit.

On Mom's urging, I flew to Hawai'i to persuade HBF to settle. I emulated him by getting drunk myself and throwing up into exotic plants on the grounds of the Royal Hawaiian Hotel.

JBFand me, early 1959, in Honolulu,
putting on happy faces wile I talked him
into settling the civil lawsuit

What possible grounds for defense did HBF have? He wanted to claim that my pal had threatened him. Since HBF was holding the gun, that probably wouldn't have worked well.

HBF settled, selling Orcas Island Airport to the county in order to pay the $10,000 to my poor friend's family. That solved the problem of the notoriety that a civil suit would have provided.

"Look, there's a positive side to this: you don't have to work your boyfriend through graduate school; let your father do it," someone tried to console me. It didn't work; I was inconsolable.

THE STATE OF WASHINGTON, Plaintiff,
vs.
HAROLD B. FERRIS
Defendant.

No. 1981

INFORMATION

Comes now _____ Elmon A. Genasta _____, Prosecuting Attorney, in and for _____ SanJuan _____ County, State of Washington, in the name and by the authority of the State of Washington, and by this his information accuses _____ Harold B. Ferris _____

of the crime of _____ Assault in the Second Degree _____

_____ RCW 9.11.020 Subsection 51 _____ committed as follows, to-wit:

That the said _____ Harold B. Ferris _____

in the County of _____ SanJuan _____ State of Washington, on or about the _____ 24th _____

day of _____ August _____ 1958, did then and there being unlawfully and feloniously

COUNTY OF WHATCOM

THE STATE OF WASHINGTON to the Sheriff of San Juan County, Washington,

WHEREAS, HAROLD B. FERRIS has been duly convicted in the Superior Court of the State of Washington for said County, of the crime of Assault in the Third Degree and Judgment has been pronounced against him, and the Court having decreed that he be punished by not more than thirty (30) days in the San Juan County Jail and that he pay the costs of this prosecution; all of which appears of record.

NOW THIS IS TO COMMAND YOU, the said Sheriff that you take the said Defendant, HAROLD B. FERRIS, and confine him in said jail as provided by law for the aforesaid term and until such costs are paid, secured or disposed of by law provided, and these presents are your authority for the same; HEREIN FAIL NOT.

WITNESS the Honorable Bert Kale, Judge of said Superior Court and the Seal thereof, this 15th day of July, 1960.

Harry O. Loft
County Clerk and ex-officio Clerk
of the Superior Court of the State
of Washington in and for Whatcom
County.

What happened to HBF on the criminal charges?

Fifty-two summers later, in 2013, I found the court records. They showed what Dad faced back in 1958.

The criminal case dragged on and on, with changes of venue to nearby Whatcom County.

COURT RECORDS, in two counties, showed HBF put up an enormous fight to stay out of jail, which would have meant--but for plea bargaining --losing his cherished master's license and job with Matson.

Eventually, through plea bargaining, HBF was allowed to plead guilty to second-degree assault in San Juan County, serve 30 days in the county jail, then to return to Whatcom County and change his plea to not guilty of third-degree assault, a lesser charge.

He served his time, officially unbeknownst to Matson, while on paid vacation from his company during the summer of 1959.

HBF never talked with me about his time in jail. But from others' reports, it's unlikely that it was good times as usual. His friend and drinking companion, Harold Jensen, died that summer, a sad time for both the Jensen and Ferris couples.

Friends from Orcas helped, without condoning his criminal action. Thad and Mary McGlinn decided that the jail mattresses were too hard, and found him a better one. They, Mom, Wayne and Esther Johnson, and others frequently came to play bridge and gab. Because the jail didn't have a kitchen, HBF was allowed to take his meals at the restaurant down the street.

When he returned to Matson, he was given his old ship, the Hawaiian Craftsman, which he mastered for the next five years. Altogether, after his big failure, he put in a thirteen-year stint with the company.

Grieving the loss of family, possible family, and friends, and not wanting to testify against HBF in court, I left the Bellingham job for San Francisco, where I went into intensive psychoanalysis for two years. I unloaded anger, frustration, self-pity, and guilt, the latter over having slapped HBF, for instance, and over whether the contents of my private diary had caused his excessive drinking or the aggression against my fiance.

Through the San Francisco Psychoanalytic Society, I obtained a reduced rate, which I paid myself, and a psychiatrist whom, I soon discovered, I could drive into uncontrollable fits of sneezing by coming up with juicy details.

I found some good reporting and editing jobs and some lesser ones, and made some life-long friends. Eventually I met a caring man, married him, settled into some happy decades as a wife and mother, and practiced forgiveness of self and others until, thankfully, it became almost habit.

I have maintained a life-long aversion to having guns around the house. In an ideal world, where nobody drinks habitually and excessively, guns might not be an issue. Dad's failure was one of failing to recognize or defeat his enemy-- alcohol--until it caught up with him and threatened four lives: those of my friend, my mother, HBF, and my own.

CHAPTER 10: Finished With Engines

Dad retired in 1968, at the usual age: 65. He never quit drinking. He did cut back, to one or two Scotches after dinner, or during bridge, at which he and Mom gained life-time master's points.

While I was working with a group of dietitians on a published project I'd originated, I talked Mom into feeding HBF crackers and cheese when he drank. This cut the effects somewhat.

Quitting drinking at that stage might not have helped his mental outlook anyway. He found new ways to be obnoxious to younger generations. Due to his racial and ethnic views, he refused to attend either my wedding in 1962 (husband Jewish), or, a few years later, that of the man he mentored (wife Asian).

My husband and I felt compassion for him, along with deep sympathy for Mom, who dealt patiently with so much unacceptable behavior.

Dr. Karl Moran, who came from Orcas to San Francisco to give me away at my wedding, and his wife, Mary, convinced HBF to let my mother come to Boston when our first child was born, in 1966.

A few years later, they sold most of the land that Mom had accumulated and inherited. They learned passable Spanish before setting off on an automobile trip across Mexico, west to east, to find a village where they could house their friends, daughter and spouse, and grandchildren.

For the next decade, they spent winters in the Yucatan Peninsula, towing a boat behind their latest car, on annual journeys from Orcas to rented mansions in or near the Mayan village of Chicxulub,

ANASTASIO PECHE, Dad's Mayan friend, above at left with Thad McGlinn and his wife Mary (back to camera)

There, he found a fishing companion, Anastasio Peche, with whom he fished for rubia--which make tasty ceviche when marinated in lime juice--off the Yucatan Peninsula. Anastasio also traveled to Orcas for a few summers to look for salmon in upper Puget Sound.. Friends from Orcas visited Chicxulub, and my husband and sons came for a few Christmases. Most of my writing income went to fly us back and forth among Boston, Orcas, and Chicxulub.

HBF became proud of my marathonning and writing career when a good publisher issued the health calendar I'd invented, one that out-sold later ones by Jim Fixx and Jane Fonda for three years and had a publishing life of more than a decade.[29] When HBF and Mom were driving along a highway and saw a jogger, he'd lean out and yell, "Sell 'em a book!"

---

[29] EAT & RUN. Jan Ferris Koltun. NY: Holt, 1975-85

Somewhere in the Sixties he traded land, now known as "The Ditch," for a yacht, with which he took charter parties to Alaska in the summers.

He and my mother sold their big house, which now is an excellent bed and breakfast. Mom named the smaller place "FWE." or "Finished With Engines." They put up a double-wide trailer on their beach acre. I later inherited it, sold it, built another house, helped to restore the littoral, then sold the property.

During month-long family summer vacations on Orcas, my mother cooked us magnificent meals from the extensive garden that Dad weeded. My husband and I and our children went with HBF and Virginia on boating and fishing trips in Canada, but he never showed his bigoted aspect to my husband, probably because he didn't want us to desert him completely.

A RETIREMENT TREK with HBF's protégé, Capt. Robert Johnson.

FISHING NEAR ALERT BAY with Wes Langell's grandson, Leo, aka the "Bilge Bunny." On the back of this photo, HBF wrote: "This fish weighed 70 pounds when caught, but it lost ten pounds by the time it arrived at the scales."

HBF built a tree house for my sons. It featured a cannon that fired real tennis balls. He also bought them motorized scooters, which they loved until they found it was too expensive to take them back to Boston at summer's end. After a year in which my writing income enabled my marital family to rent a nearby house, HBF and Mom built us a guest house.

What else did he do, besides weeding vegetables and taking friends and family on cruises, during the FWE period?

He found, to his astonishment, that he was a water witch. When he and Roger Purdue, a class-mate of Mom's who owned the falling-down garage in Eastsound, went out to search for new water sources for the village, Roger allowed him to try his dowsing rods. Bingo! HBF pin-pointed artesian wells, west of the airport, that served the area for several years. After that discovery, he served on the Eastsound Water Board.

He bought a bulldozer, and sent a photo he made of it to our sons with the caption, "Men's toys cost more than boys'". Then he mired it in the marsh behind FWE, and sold it.

He played the organ, at least in the summers. The table next to his organ was graced by a two-foot-tall black stone bear. He'd acquired it when he and Mom were rafted next to another yacht in Princess Louisa because the dock was full that week. The couple on the next boat were drunk and fighting over the wife's taste in art. The husband came out on their afterdeck, carrying the bear in his arms to throw it overboard.

Dad was alarmed. Princess Louisa's waters are 2,000 feet deep in that area, so the bear would have been lost forever. "Hold off," he told the man. "I'll give you $100 for it."

Later, the bear was appraised and found to be an Inuit dancing bear, much more valuable than HBF's offer.

Next-door neighbors, part-time islanders, recall that every time they arrived on North Beach they were introduced to Dad's "to do" list, made out especially for them. He took them to the Bellingham Yacht Club for a thank-you lunch, which couldn't possibly have paid for all the done "to dos."

It was about that time that he shot up the chicken coop. He was becoming concerned that a raccoon was eating chickens, so he rigged up an electronic device, connected to the birds' home and to the nightstand by his bed. One night, the neighbors heard a barrage of gunfire. Wisely, they stayed indoors.

The next morning, they found that he hadn't gotten the raccoon but had "shot the shit out of the chicken house roof." Fortunately for his relations with Mom, he didn't kill any chickens.

He fished a bit, and bought a smoker. After a trip into Canada in 1980, when I caught a huge salmon, Mom suggested I obtain Dad's recipe for the brine in which he marinated fish before smoking them overnight.

"He won't be around forever, you know," she said.

In his handwriting, the recipe sits in my cookbook:

1/2 salt, 1/2 brown sugar
Marinate for three hours. Take out of brine. Rinse in fresh water. Air dry on paper towels for one hour.
Change racks[30].

He won two contests from the *Sunset* feature, Chefs of the West. Here is one of the recipes published in their cookbook:

ORCAS ISLAND SCRAPPLE Capt. Hal Ferris, master mariner, Eastsound, Washington

2 pounds pork odds and ends (knuckles, hocks, etc.)
1/2 clove garlic
2 stalks celery with leaves
1 bunch parsley
1 pinch sage
salt and pepper to taste
2 cups medium-grind oatmeal

Put all ingredients except the oatmeal in a 3-quart kettle; cover with cold water and simmer for about 2 hours, or until the pork falls off the bones. Remove bones, celery, and parsley, and gradually stir in the oatmeal. Cook slowly, stirring constantly and watching the mixture carefully to prevent burning.

When it is about the consistency of thick mush, pour it into bread pans and let it stand for 2 to 3 hours to cool. Then cut into 1/8 or 1/4-inch slices and saute in bacon drippings over low to medium heat until crisp and golden brown. Serve with currant jelly, fried apples, or apple butter.

Encouraged by the success of his recipes, he joined a writing class and worked on his own autobiographical essays, including the one on Josie, and another about his experiences in Tahiti with acupuncture. I edited his unpublished work lightly, to improve the signals-to-noise ratios. Along with his 1933-34 sailing logs that Mom had typed, and possibly revised, I used the writings in this manuscript, and preserved the originals.

He came to appreciate women's skills in boat management, especially those of my mother. He admired Bob

---

[30] This may refer to changing the salmon's position in the smoker, where he used apple wood to provide smoke overnight.

Eagan's wife, whom HBF called "Captain Josephine" because she capably ran the Park Service boat from Sucia to Smuggler's Cove, aka "The Ditch."

HBF joined the Episcopal Church, where for several years he raised the flags on the parish lawn Sunday mornings. He particularly enjoyed Rev. Glion T. Benson, who had himself been a merchant mariner, and who expressed reliance on "Buda," the engine in his boat. I believe Fr. Benson and the other parishioners helped HBF to understand that while he was unquestionably captain of his fate, a greater power was master of his soul.

He and my mother left thousands of photos, newspaper clippings, letters, stories, and artifacts, which I've used to write, edit, and make this book. I hope you've enjoyed reading it as much as I've enjoyed having the last word on my Old Man.

Ships HBF Served or Mastered

Matson personnel records and HBF's own recollections indicate that he served on 48 ships, not including the sailing vessels Nomad and Viking, nor the Corsair and Newport, small yachts he owned during retirement. He served as master on 17 ships; the latter, below, are starred.

Admiral Fiske
*Alameda
Camden
Chateau Thiery
City of Los Angeles
*DM Dickensen
General Sherman
Golden Cloud
Golden Harvest
Golden State
*Hawaiian Builder
*Hawaiian Craftsman
*Hawaiian Fisherman
*Hawaiian Planter
*Hawaiian Refiner
*Joseph Lane
*JT McMillan
Lurline
Makawao
Makua
Maliko
Malolo
Mana
Manini
Manoa
Manui

Manukai
Manulani
Manulei
Mapele
*Marine Flasher
Mariposa
*Mark Hopkins
Matsonia
Maui
Mauna Ala
Mauna Loa
Maunawili
Monterey
North Haven
Pennsylvanian
President Harding
*Rensselaer Victory
*Sea Centaur
*Sierra
*Sonoma
*Thomas Hart Benton
*WB Ayer

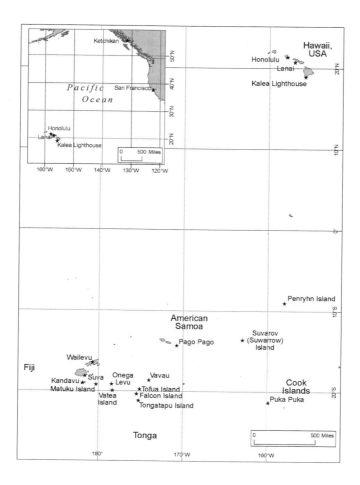

Voyage One, 1933--Nomad: Suva, Fiji to San Francisco. Map courtesy of
Nancy Alexander, ndigart@gmail.com